Activate Your Pineal Gland

An Essential Guide About the Third Eye Awakening and Achieving Spiritual Enlightenment

Amber V. Robbins

ROSE
TRIFOLIA PRESS

acknowledge that the author is not engaging in the rendering of legal, financial, medical or professional advice. The content within this book has been derived from various sources. Please consult a licensed professional before attempting any techniques outlined in this book.

By reading this document, the reader agrees that under no circumstances are the author or the publisher responsible for any losses, direct or indirect, which are incurred as a result of the use of the information contained within this document, including, but not limited to, — errors, omissions, or inaccuracies.

ISBN: Print 978-1-955661-07-2

Ebook 978-1-955661-08-9

Table of Contents

SPECIAL BONUS

Want this Bonus Book for <u>FREE</u>?

Get <u>FREE</u>, unlimited access to it and all of my new books by joining my Fan Base!

Scan with your camera to join!

Introduction

<u>Who Is the Author?</u>

Hi, I'm Amber.

As a qualified natural healer, fitness trainer, and overall health advocate, I seek to improve the wellbeing of my readers. With over 20 years of experience in leading people to find happiness through means of a healthy and spiritual lifestyle, I intend to provide through this book a guide to those searching for deeper healing and intuitive growth.

The personal experience of spiritual awakening is such a personally fulfilling process that the only thing I enjoy more is helping others reach their highest self. Consistent learning and practice have been essential for me to maintain my skill of helping others and to spread essential knowledge. Teachers also need new knowledge, just like leaders still need continuous direction.

I conclude this short introduction with a quote I love: *"The shaman's duty is to dissolve boundaries between order and disorder, to promote healing, cleansing, purification, and a realignment of the spirit in a world where there is chaos, toxicity, and disproportionate living, thinking, feeling, and being."* - *Hyman, 2007, p.10*

Why Was This Book Written?

"A light bulb is capable of shining light on the room around it but not on the power which illuminates it. In the same way, we're capable of comprehending the world around us but not the consciousness which animates us." - *Dada Gunamuktananda*

If you open any of your social media apps, turn on the news, or watch the latest Netflix series you would catch a glimpse of our spiritual crisis as a species. As human beings, we continuously separate ourselves from the rest of the universe and make the assumption that we are the most special and superior species in existence. While this can be true in some sense, this thought is not entirely accurate. Our idea of intelligence can only be measured within the scale of human capability, according to our own understanding of the concept. A famous quote from Albert

Einstein explains this perfectly, that "if you determine a fish's intelligence by its ability to climb a tree, it will continue its life believing that it is stupid."

Our idea of intelligence is subjective. Even the understanding of the definition itself depends on how intelligent you think you are. Where someone can call you a smart person, they might not be judging you as harshly as they would someone else. As humans we truly can never know if we are actually intelligent, because the knowledge held by you or me is reflective of or only logical to ourselves. You might call yourself an intelligent person, but beware. You are probably letting your ego get the best of you in that moment and are unaware you're even doing so.

There is a layer of your consciousness that is oftentimes neglected. The cost is at the expense of having a correct understanding of reality. However, if you can see the true picture before you instead of what you want to believe, this goes past intelligence and enters a layer of the mind known as wisdom. Wisdom can be seen as a navigator, which aims our intellect in the right direction. Our virtues stem from our wisdom as well, as you can witness those virtues being something that manifests from the deeper processes (subconscious) of the mind. If you want to throw a metaphor at this idea, think of intellect as a great eye, whereas wisdom is the muscle that allows the eye to move in your desired direction. Wisdom is obtained through objective experience and self-reflection, which can depend on both the external and internal factors of your life.

If you can rework your mind to absorb this understanding of wisdom and intellect, then it is possible to gain a better understanding of the full spectrum of your mind and the areas that may need greater attention. The danger with intellect is that it can potentially overshadow your wisdom, diminishing our efforts to navigate this reality in the best manner possible. To avoid such a debacle, we need to balance these twin aspects of the mind and apply both the necessary exercises and practices in order to be successful.

We are made of the matter that exists around us that stretches past the boundaries of planet Earth and into the secretive Universe. There are some open-minded individuals that refer to themselves as "star children" and "star souls", which are believed to be unique individuals that carry special perceptive abilities that aren't available to the average human being. These people are thought to be the descendants of the constellations and the stars themselves. Some even go as far as to say they are inter-dimensional beings. While these terms are metaphysical concepts and don't carry any actual scientific weight, they are still used within everyday society by ordinary people. Indeed, this belief has some supporting evidence that verifies that we are composed of the same elements and materials that compose the stars, specifically stars that underwent a supernova explosion. This puts into perspective how connected we are to the universe outside of our own planet, albeit on an atomic or quantum level. As mysterious as this phenomenon sounds, it can be untangled through scientific methods. Even our DNA has been found in its cross-section as the flower of life, adhering to the naturally occurring "golden ratio". The same principle or ratio can be found in the refraction of light and sound, as well as ancient writings, whose secrets are yet to be revealed.

As humans we are capable to draw meaning from our life experiences through our senses (sometimes referred to as sensory instruments, which include sight, smell, taste, hearing, and touch). What's more is that we can differentiate these senses from our conscious thoughts, intelligence vs. intellect. This ability allows us to be much more than a mere flesh and bone vessel with the primary goal of survival.

Fortunately, there is an increasing number of people that discover the advantages of spiritual growth and also understand the necessity of passing on their knowledge. Since you bought this book, you are one of those people and your contribution can actively help society and people grow into more empathetic and aware beings.

What Will You Learn from this Book?

We are creatures that are attracted to new and shiny things. Basically, we are like ostriches with anxiety, right? Our objective in life should be to find happiness, healing, and growth. Sometimes we try to artificially fill our life with material objects, vain pursuits, and the immediate pleasures of the flesh. Trying to live a happy life by way of materialism and ego sets a standard in which you will be running around in circles. You'll find yourself needing more, the next iPhone, the newest Gucci slides, a bigger house, expensive cars, anything to scratch that "instant gratification" itch. This loop of destruction will only bring you to a morbid life full of regret and despair, which you will only recognize once it's too late.

Your life goal should be to find a purpose, a deep meaning. The purpose of your life does not necessarily mean that you are required to provide massive contributions to society or for the greater good, but simply that your purpose allows you to be satisfied with your life. When are you truly rich? When you are happy with your lot.

This book will be a step towards your awakening to a new world of observation and contemplation. You may even feel for the first time that your feeling of belonging as a human, being an equal actor in the world, will be acknowledged and explained. Using the following information as your guide, you can learn ways of correctly achieving and maintaining spiritual enlightenment, using methods that won't come as a shock to your system, or ask you to reconsider everything you've ever thought. The teachings you'll find in this book are all about organic principles, inherent truths in your life as a spiritual being. This will open many doors of higher consciousness and will provide your spiritual engine with a tune up via the natural and divine world that we call our home. Simple daily habits and healthy practices can help you to reactivate your possibly dormant pineal gland and thus open your third eye.

Starting out with the basics, I will take you back

into the history and symbolic significance of the pineal gland. You will learn the function of the pineal gland within the body and why it relates to your third eye. The advantages of harnessing this power will directly affect your body, mind, and spirit. It is essential that you, as the reader, adjust your daily routine and spiritual practices in order to achieve your end goal of enlightenment.

Disclaimer

This book has been designed as guide that will answer questions such as: What is the pineal gland? What is its relationship to the third eye? How can you awaken this third eye? In your quest to gain answers to these questions you will need to learn a few daily practices and meditations that will help you deepen your knowledge and reach your goal.

However, this book should not be used as a substitute for medical issues like depression, anxiety, or paranoia. You should always consult the advice from a registered medical professional if you suspect you're in bad health or are suffering from a medical or psychological condition. Please consult your doctor or physician before following the practices from this book.

By participating in these daily physical practices, I assume you are aware of all the risks associated with exercises of this nature. All yoga poses and the other workouts should be performed in a safe and supervised environment. Your sessions should include an adequate warm-up and cool-down.

Chapter 1: The Basics

"This is how magic is done. By hurling yourself into the abyss and discovering it's a feather bed." - Terence McKenna

In order to understand the main topics we will discuss, we will have a look at the concept of higher consciousness and the function of your pineal gland in achieving this state of mind. How this organ interplays with the daily functions and exceptional abilities of the rest of your brain and body is a rather weighty subject. The hope is that it all these aspects of you will come together in a spiritual equilibrium.

The overall experience of consciousness is a mysterious phenomenon, even more so the experience of a higher self, which is vaguely interconnected with the conscious and subconscious parts of your mind. To decipher and better manage what happens in your unconscious mind can pave the way towards discovering your higher consciousness. The physical source of these possibilities brings us to the discussion about your pineal gland.

The pineal gland is a pea-sized, pinecone-shaped endocrine organ that is situated in the geometric center of your brain, between the right and left hemispheres. This organ regulates your sleep-wake patterns by rhythmically producing melatonin (an indoleamine hormone that is involved in our biological rhythms). In turn, this determines your hormone levels, stress regulation, immune response, and physical performance on a daily and seasonal basis. As you can imagine, these effects are critical for the optimal functioning of your entire mind-body system.

From an evolutionary standpoint, your pineal and retinal photoreceptor cells have functional similarities. Your retina's main purpose is to receive and convert light into neural signals and send these signals to the brain for visual recognition. In fact, there is a rather direct neural pathway between your retina and the pineal gland, and it is these neural pathways that can determine our instinctive reactions towards events in our daily lives and how we process information.

A more body-based description of the retina's process is that the images we see arrive at the pineal gland through a complex multi-neuronal pathway that begins in our retina. The first stop on this pathway is from the retina to the central nervous system within what is scientifically known as the retinohypothalamic tract. From there, the central nervous system goes into the lateral hypothalamus, where neural pathways continue to move towards the spinal cord and the superior cervical ganglions (Pevet, 2019, p.16).

Even though your pineal gland is linked to the retina, it seems that over time we, mammals, have started to lose our acute photosensitive ability. This is why you will need to focus on practices to train your organ to harness this ability. You should consider building the brain to be no different from physically training your body. For example, a bodybuilder needs to focus and build each and every muscle group individually in order to gain well-rounded strength, guaranteeing that the body is balanced. Should any muscle group be neglected, then the bodybuilder could start to experience muscle and joint pains, or worst of all, injure himself.

Luckily, you won't experience these joint or muscle pains in the pineal gland, but the truth is that the brain needs to be trained with the same idea in mind. In order to utilize the brain to its full capacity and potential, it needs to be trained on a regular basis. This is particularly true for the pineal gland. The more training you have, the deeper the brains pathways become, and the more connected you will be to your pineal gland's abilities.

Connection Between the Pineal Gland and the Third Eye

It is not only in the modern day that we are trying to reconnect with our spirituality. The effort undergoes a renaissance in every age. We see not only individuals, but entire communities wanting to return to a simplistic, although spiritually evolved, way of life. Across various cultures, today and throughout history, there have been multiple endeavors to reach a higher level of consciousness. The question is, where do we find our higher consciousness on a physical level?

An important distinction that you should note, about the mind-body system, is that consciousness cannot necessarily be pinpointed to a single region in the body. Some say it must be in our brain, as we often describe our thoughts in relation to this organ. Others have said we experience feelings in our core or down our spinal cord. Observing these experiences gives us insight into how interconnected consciousness is with the body and mind of each human being. A basic practice of internal observation can give you a better understanding of this principle. Close your eyes and try to focus on the quality and character of your thoughts. You may notice that your thoughts aren't geographically located in your head, like they have no forwarding address. This is because your thoughts manifest in a portion of your mind that you cannot locate, much like a transparent arch over your head.

Now let's take it one step further. Try and locate the point from which you consciously experience. Go ahead. Start by slowly navigating and tuning into the regions of your head, chest, gut, and pelvis at your own pace. What you may notice is that you activate these regions by placing your awareness on them. If you continue the practice and focus harder, you will become aware that these regions become the reference point of conscious experience. Don't try and activate your pelvis through the region of your head. Instead try to experience the temperature, sensations, and space in and around your pelvis. You'll find that consciousness does not have a fixed position in the body.

Similarly, the point from which your conscious experience appears cannot be found. Moreover, we are able to consciously observe, and attend to, emotions that arise throughout any moment in our lives. We also have the capacity to manage the reactions that emerge before the half-life of an emotion. There is a definitive connection between our physical and emotional reactions. For example, there have been cases where severe emotional trauma has caused the sufferer's heartstrings to rip, literally "dying of a broken heart". Recognition and understanding of these factors are crucial for our health. We can only navigate these emotions and reactions skillfully and correctly if we are informed and experienced.

The connection between the pineal gland and our third eye serves as the physical manifestation of our thoughts, feelings, and spirituality. This is because your pineal gland is the organ that receives neural inputs to ultimately determine how we feel and perceive our reality. It takes great effort and attention to nourish this organ in order to better regulate both your physical and spiritual health.

Taking the third eye into consideration, we must remember that what we experience spiritually not just centered in the self but becomes a part of our communities. Our environment and the people around us contribute to what you can refer to as the "collective" consciousness. As soon as this realization truly occurs, the idea of our existence expands far past the immediate physical space we occupy. You'll find that your happiness and contentment is actually influenced by the dynamics of communal/collective participation and growth. Our happiness should not depend on some individualistic lifestyle that we are being conditioned to live by nowadays through external factors like social media, advertisements, financial services, and fashion, to name a few.

Hidden Secrets

The abilities of the pineal gland were studied long before we could find evidence of its exact functions. Harnessing its mystical powers was a prominent practice all over the world for centuries. The significance of the pineal gland's shape, that of a pinecone, can be found in many spiritual and religious practices throughout history.

The spines of a pinecone spiral are perfect, fulfilling the "golden ratio" of the Fibonacci sequence, which is also referred to as Sacred Geometry (a naturally occurring ratio of expanding geometric patterns). This divine mathematic ratio has led to the pineal gland being regarded as one of the most ancient and sacred symbols, as the seed that feeds our souls.

It is interesting to see just how prominent this symbol is within our own past, especially because it mostly goes unnoticed in today's modern landscape. In the past many representations of this symbol were hidden in other visuals, perhaps to ensure that its powers were only available to mystical, holy, or learned members of society. Nowadays, our pinecone shaped pineal glands are being further investigated by those seeking spiritual enlightenment.

Ancient Remnants and Older

Discoveries

The Latin root of the word pineal, *pinea*, means "pinecone". This refers to the outer shape of the gland, but if you were to cut it open, the gland resembles the shape of an eye. Many symbols and discoveries from the past are linked to the pineal gland.

Ancient Assyrian carvings dating all the way back to 700 B.C depict a pinecone pollinating the tree of life. This is a tribute to the pinecone's symbolism of immortality.

Buddhists shaped their hair into a pinecone spiral to honor the powers of the pineal gland. They have perfected the meditative practice of non-verbal expression in order to embody the natural mind.

In the Persian architecture, we see the importance of incorporating Sacred Geometric patterns from nature into their man-made infrastructure and decor. According to the Persian culture, geometry has a ritual purpose, the sacred nature of numbers reflecting the perfection of the universe and creation.

The history of the implementation of Sacred Geometry by man goes back countless generations (Hejazi, 2004, p.1). If you look at the Egyptian Staff of Osiris (1224 B.C) you'll notice that it is made from two intertwining serpents that move upwards towards a pinecone. The eye of Horus represents the five senses, with the additional sense of *thought,* and it is this exact symbol that can be found in a cross-section of the brain known as the "corpus callosum" or "brainstem". The eye of Horus resembles the lateral view of the pineal gland and is illustrated on the foreheads of Egyptian sarcophagi.

The Coat of Arms of the Holy See found on the Vatican flag depicts three crowns stacked in the shape of a pinecone. In Vatican City you can even find a statue of a pinecone that was originally next to an Egyptian temple in the ancient Rome. In the Catholic Church you can also see the burning of incense used to manifest spiritual energy or the cleansing of holy places.

The Indian (Kundalini) and Mexican (Chicomecoati) deities are also frequently accompanied by serpents, the third eye, and pinecones. These are meant to be offerings.

The Sumerian gods, believed to be the *Anunnaki* (an advanced and ancient extraterrestrial race that visited Earth), are depicted in carvings holding a pinecone in one hand. This race of beings is referred to in connection to the modern study of the "reptilian brain", the section of our brain associated with instinct.

The Hindu god, Shiva, has three eyes. The third eye is the symbol of intellect, awakening, and enlightenment that will destroy all the evil and ignorance in its path. In addition to this, Shiva's third eye also has the ability to see into higher dimensions of existence.

The 17th-century philosopher, scientist, and mathematician René Descartes dedicated his studies towards our human consciousness. He believed that the pineal gland is the "principal seat of the soul" and is our link between the physical and spiritual worlds. This is the philosopher who coined the famous line, *"I think, therefore I am"*.

Herophilus (325–280 BC), the Greek father of anatomy, considered the pineal gland to be our well of memory. It was already at this very early stage that the pineal gland was clearly understood to be an instrument involved with a deeper consciousness.

Modern-Day

According to Yogic tradition, our *chakras* are the energy centers of our bodies. Chakras collect and pass on *prana* (life force energy). Our material bodies could not exist without them, because they serve as the gateways for the flow of energy and life into our physical bodies (Bhetiwal, 2017, p. 1556).

Today, the third eye is associated with the sixth chakra (Ajna) and represents "inner sight". It is considered to be our most powerful source of ethereal energy. Balancing all the chakras is necessary to achieve a healthy spiritual and mental stability. We continuously learn that time spent in the sunshine, sleeping in complete darkness, and returning to organic foods and drinking more water have significantly positive effects on the mind-body system.

It was only in the 1950s that we discovered that melatonin synthesis in the pineal gland is much higher during the night, and this led to it being referred to as the "biochemical expression of darkness". Even more interestingly, contrary to the rest of the brain, the pineal gland is not isolated from the rest of the body and receives copious amounts of blood flow.

In modern science, we are fortunate enough to have several experts that can express the connection between our physical and spiritual realms by means of their education, training, and study in psychology, neurology, philosophy, and biology.

Dr. Ashok Panagariya, a neurologist in Jaipur, says that "the most astounding discovery of all is that the brain produces a parapsychology enhancing neurotransmitter". In plain English, your brain has the potential to tap into the energy of other realms through a class of brain substances known as beta-carbolines. These are neurochemicals produced by the pineal gland and, according to Dr. Panagariya, are only produced during the night and break down your melatonin, a substance that has been linked to psychic episodes (Iqbal, 2013).

Apart from the rhythmic production of melatonin, there are many more brain discharges to take into account: the ultradian rhythm, the infradian rhythm, and the seasonal rhythm. For people living at the North Pole, during the never-ending darkness of winter, melatonin secretion is at its peak numbers. These changes are what give birds their almost supernatural ability to predict future weather and wind patterns. For mammals, melatonin allows them to seasonally hibernate, regulate their body temperatures, and control their reproduction timelines (Bruce & Macchi, 2004, p.177).

There is also an emerging field of study referred to as "big history", a unified study of all the fields involved in our understanding of the history of our universe (although, it is rather like shooting blind, as we are the ones doing the writing and our knowledge of the history of the entire cosmos is, of course, limited). It is specifically within Geology that we may find the link between humans and the cosmos. Rocks have memory. They have the ability to record the conditions, the surrounding history, by which they are consistently formed. These conditions include specific temperatures, the pressure in the atmosphere, and the effect of other elements in the same area. Looking into the lives of rocks actually helped scientists come to the conclusion that we are made of the same compounds as those found in a supernova.

Chapter 2: Awakening

"And those who were seen dancing were thought to be insane by those who could not hear the music." - Friedrich Nietzsche

Are you achieving enlightenment or are you driving yourself crazy?

There is an open stigma around mental illness. What is even crazier is that some people with spiritual gifts are labeled as broken or clinically insane. People often demonize what they don't understand. The worst distance between two people is misunderstanding, caused by emotional unintelligence, ignorance, and fear. Let's not forget about the long history of "witch" prosecution. Many women were sent to the hangman's rope because they did things women weren't expected or even forbidden to do, like holistic healing, or having a strong voice.

Unfortunately, some people today are quick to dismiss spiritual practices and enlightenment, finding that it doesn't have enough scientific backing to be considered accurate or effective. These are the quick assumptions of the uneducated, delusional, and disconnected from reality. Our greatest loss as a species would be to no longer follow spiritual insight that has continued to propel us forward into new ages of meaning for thousands of years. Even worse, some try to convince those who have spiritual perceptions that they are completely skewed, then force upon them ideologies and concepts that cheapen their experience of existence.

Would you send a dog to a psychiatric hospital because it barks instead of speak English? You could try to teach the dog to speak English, but still, it continues to bark. So, you sedate it with drugs and slap a "clinically insane" badge on its forehead because it can't speak English. Exaggerations aside, there are methods that we can use so that we are better equipped to take care of these spiritual individuals so that they can be set on the correct path. For all we know, this might be the most salient thing to do for humanity's future.

We neglect the fact that we need to further develop existing spiritual systems and archetypes that have already been discovered, documented, and shared. We have scriptures, texts, and works from numerous religious backgrounds and philosophic traditions from across various cultures around the world that have nurtured human spirituality for centuries. Nevertheless, we still require continuous contribution, and refinement in these various forms of spiritual knowledge and rituals, so that we can achieve the awakening that can be shared by all. Spirituality, in all its different interpretations and definitions, needs to become a mandatory need, no different than having to drink water and eat food every day. Through spirituality, it is possible for us to reach awakenings in the everyday moments of our lives. We can create a human race that is more connected, sophisticated, and appreciative of the reality we live in and the present we all experience, regardless of where each of us is coming from.

It is a guiding principle of Indigenous tribes to provide unconditional support for their fellow men, providing mentorship throughout their awakening. Having your consciousness expanded and learning lost truths can be overwhelming on the mind as well as the body, especially if it arises suddenly and without proper preparation. Still, it is worth mentioning that mental illness should also not be ignored and instead properly treated, but keep in mind that there is more out there than pills to treat mental illness.

Advantages and Dangers of an Open Third Eye

Spiritual awakenings can strengthen your intuition, helping you to detect aspects of your relationships that may have a negative impact on your "self". Even potential dangers in social environments may become clearer, as you are more acutely aware of your surroundings. Part of this is to accept that you might lose connections with a few people as their true colors come to light. It could potentially save you from years of emotional and mental suffering (imagine dealing with narcissists and sociopaths your entire life without even knowing it. How draining!) and ever-growing feelings of loneliness.

These feelings easily become embedded and cause unconscious trauma, which damages our ability to be spiritually in tune. There is a famous quote by Robin Williams that sums up this idea pretty perfectly. He said that he used to think the worst thing in life was to end up all alone, but it is not. The worst thing in life will be to end up with people that make you feel alone.

There are forgotten truths about yourself that you will discover, and this can have a staggering effect on your mind. Having your sense of self completely altered is something that has to be gradually accepted and then accordingly applied to your life in order to strengthen the new qualities that are just now entering your world. Getting accustomed to a new identity of openness requires an attentive and healthy process that cannot be rushed.

One can easily confuse awakening with an inflated ego in the beginning. Since you are gaining possession of wisdom that others around might not possess themselves, it is important that this newly gained wisdom be used as a mean to improve the lives of others and yourself. It is not spiritually right to place all your energy solely on the "self". You won't be able to move forward in your path of awakening until you are capable of separating your ego from reality. Your ego can be used as a tool rather than an identity. Stepping into the realm of the ego and entertaining it with your attention will close the doors of awakening that you are eagerly trying to open and reverse the progress you have made. Observing the ego and choosing not to indulge in its power, is in fact a powerful position in which you find yourself. This becomes more evident and easier to practice with time.

A common occurrence among people who seek to open their third eye as quickly as possible is that they lack the patience needed and usually follow incomplete steps. This ultimately leads to either the third eye not opening or a much too overwhelming experience for the mind to handle. There have been reports of people having sleep paralysis and feeling physically sick in social situations after forcing the experience of awakening on an uneducated and ill-prepared mind.

The possibility of an activated third eye damaging the psyche can also cause the development of delusions and obsessive behavior. This can lead you to a misinterpretation of what awakening entails and could be discouraging for further pursuit or even for healing the unwanted effects. These unsavory behaviors that may develop will also negatively impact your relationships, as healthy as they might have been beforehand. Having to deal with a damaged psyche as well as a feeling of abandonment can be utterly crushing to your goals of enlightenment.

If your understanding of reality gets completely turned around, it is crucial that you find an anchor of familiarity. What some people refer to as the "matrix" is still very much the reality of most individuals, and there is nothing wrong with keeping a grasp on your roots. We are human animals after all. The anchor that you can find is part of a technique referred to as *grounding*, which will be discussed in the following chapter.

As an exemplification of why having an anchor is important, you can read about Adam Gentry. Adam Gentry had a psychotic break that led to his institutionalization and "treatment" with all kinds of Western medications. Adam's story was featured in a documentary directed by Phil Borges, called *Crazywise* (2017). Unlike the shamans of indigenous tribes, when Gentry experienced a spiritual awakening, he was not hailed as a spiritual leader. He was thrown in a padded cell and prescribed 15 pills a day. Borges noted in the documentary how every individual should be given a role in a community and that mental illness should be treated with compassion. When Western medicine failed, even the Eastern method of Vipassana, silent meditation, did not help Gentry. Some of his long-forgotten childhood memories resurfaced during treatment and apparently what he disclosed was enough to get him sent away for good. Not having a compassionate mentor that understood mental illness, as well as spiritual health, led to Gentry having a forced and painful healing experience through meditation. Borges' interviews helped him to not give up on the process, but still, it could have been avoided.

Signs of an Open Third Eye

You should be able to easily detect the signs of your open third eye, but these can be misinterpreted. The reason why spiritual awakening has been disregarded by modern science is that an awakening is a first-hand internal experience. There are no witnesses of your spiritual awakening; all the emotion, awareness, and intuition of your experience are subjective. Still, spiritual experiences cannot be denied since for the most part they have been had in some form and fashion throughout the entire human history.

Indications

What are some of the indications you might experience?

Strong Intuition: Your gut feeling becomes like a loud voice that can predict outcomes and other people's intentions. You can sense other people's emotions, even when they are far away. It also can involve exceptional abilities like sensing events that might happen in the future. It can also refer to an extra-sensory experience when arriving at a new place or meeting a new person.

Clairvoyance: Clairvoyance is just a large SAT word for receiving intuitive messages in the form of images or scenes playing in your mind. Literally you can visually download information in your mind. However, these images require additional knowledge so that their meaning is properly deciphered.

Clairaudience: This one is similar to clairvoyance but, instead of images, you hear calm messages in your head. These could be single phrases that might guide your choices or single words like somebody's name that needs help.

Clairsentience: This refers to physically feeling a message as a sensation. This is like the knot you feel in your stomach when entering a dangerous environment, or the all-over warmth when touching someone you truly care for.

Claircognizance: This "clair" is like having dog or horse sense. For example, when you are able to pick up new information about people and places like a stranger's personality traits, buried trauma, or hidden agendas. Animals are highly sensitive to their surroundings. You should never trust anyone your dog doesn't like.

Lucid Dreaming: This is when you experience dreams in a more vivid and realistic way, and you can even believe the events in the dream are part of your actual reality. You are completely aware of what is happening, and you may be in control of these events. Strangely enough, this can help you to deal with your real-world problems.

Heightened Senses: Opening your third eye can also make your sensory input more intense. Colors become more vivid, smells more potent, and textures feel as though you are touching them for the first time. Your sense of space and temperature will become slightly elevated. Sounds appear clearer and you will recognize other subtle sounds around you, which you could only remember hearing as a child. Ultimately, every sensory instrument will be heightened, and your mind will be more alert, but there will be a sense of tranquility in your body.

Heaviness and Pain: Sometimes enlightenment can be painful. You could develop a persistent pressure in and around the brain, which is usually accompanied by intense headaches and migraines. When you touch between your eyebrows, you should feel a pulsating and warm sensation.

Extrasensory Perception (ESP): This is also referred to as precognition and defined as an atypical perceptual ability that may allow the acquisition of non-inferential input arising from a future point in time (Marwaha & May, 2015, p.1). Basically, you know what will happen before it actually happens. Although you will have no evidence to support your theories, your intuition will be spot on.

Connection with Others and Animals: You feel a heightened kinship towards people that are closest to you, and you can communicate your feelings in a more relatable way. Because of this, animals will also be drawn to you and things like training your pet may become easier because they will more clearly understand your intentions through feelings.

Spiritual Awareness: There may be a definitive presence in and around you that could only be identified as your spirit. Other people's energies also become clearer, and you can even sense their aura.

Improved Imagination: You may notice that your creative pursuits will become more natural and enjoyable. Your imagination has broken its barriers and visualization will now become a daily practice. It is as if your childlike abilities to create new worlds at the drop of a hat are being reactivated and improved.

"Astral Travel", **"Cosmological Projection"**, or **"Remote Viewing"**: The out-of-body experience of having your spirit travel to other places or through dimensions while your physical body stays put. Most often, people will experience these phenomena during intense meditation, lucid dreaming, or having a near-death incident.

Rick Strassman, a psychiatry professor in New Mexico, thought that the pineal gland is capable of producing N,N-dimethyl-tryptamine (**DMT**, also referred to as the "spirit molecule"). DMT is an extremely powerful hallucinogen, especially under certain stress conditions like the moment of birth, the process of giving birth, or the moment before death. This molecule might be the one responsible for the near-death experiences reported by patients resuscitated after cardiac arrest. Later research found that serotonin and endogenic opioids are also involved in these hallucinatory experiences (Nichols, 2018, p.30). This phenomenon may explain the occurrences of wild out-of-body experiences.

Chapter 3: Achieving

Spiritual Enlightenment

"It is better to light a candle than to curse the darkness." - Lobsang Rampa

Awakening is the first step, and it is where you get a glimpse of what your reality can be. You had a taste of the dish, now you must learn the ingredients and the steps to create the flavor you so desire. Enlightenment is the natural, and definitely necessary next step. Having been awakened to the forgotten truths of the universe and the immense potential you hold, it is without a doubt simply irresponsible to not outline the practices to reach true enlightenment.

There are many methods and techniques as to how you can achieve spiritual enlightenment. As you now know, it is an age-old endeavor, and for the most part, achievable with the right intent and action for every person, including yourself.

First and foremost, to be successful in this quest will require healing of the mind, body, and spirit. Without a healthy mind-body system, your awakening is doomed.

Some of the biggest obstacles in activating the third eye are the physical backup of calcium in the pineal gland, an unhealthy body, and a clogged and busy mind. The goal is to implement a different daily routine into your life that will clear your energies and break down the calcium in that powerful mystery organ. This is crucial in our path to enlightenment. Tan explained (2018, p.3) the cause of calcium buildup in the pineal gland by relating it to how the calcium deposits in the pineal gland were observed in vertebrates several decades ago. Some researchers believe that pineal calcification is associated with certain endocrine diseases such as schizophrenia and diabetes. Others believe that it is a natural process and has no effects on our mental state since this process already occurs during early childhood and there are instances of it having no impact in certain mammals. Recently, studies have shown that pineal calcification can possibly jeopardize melatonin production in the human brain. This may have a direct influence on neurodegenerative diseases like Alzheimer's and Dementia.

Methods and Techniques

Acupressure

Acupressure is a famous technique used in traditional Chinese medicine. It requires a person to apply light pressure on certain points of the body to stimulate the production and flow of the desired hormones and energies. Contrary to acupuncture, in acupressure, the skin is not pierced by needles. Therefore, it can easily be done by your own hand. The pressure point referred to as the Third Eye Point (GV 24.5) is located between the eyebrows where the forehead meets the bridge of the nose. By applying gentle pressure with your second finger, you should start to feel a light pulse. Be sure to take slow breaths as you do this, to stabilize your mind and stimulate spiritual awareness. In connection with this, there is the Hundred Meeting Point (GV 20), which is located on the crown of your head, and its stimulation along with the Third Eye Point may yield the best results.

Sound healing

Sound can be a powerful tool in healing. The cells of our bodies can resonate with the sound of a voice (be it our own or of another person) or instruments (whether we use it or listen to it). Our very bones and organs can achieve resonance like a tuning fork. Sound waves are even used to break down gallstones. This means that getting our bodies musically 'in tune' can be a healing experience for both the body and the mind. A popular and effective method is drumming in unison. These repetitive sounds being made and heard as a group have wonderful effects on spiritual energy. Heather explained (2007, p.7) that the repetitive sounds of a drumbeat can fuse our heartbeat to that rhythm. In a healing session, we may even try to take a person's pulse to determine their heart rate and then begin playing at that same rate. Over a time period of ten minutes, we may gradually reduce the drumbeat to aid the person in relaxation. We can monitor the rhythm of their breathing to determine how quickly their heart rate and breathing rate have harmonized to the drumbeat.

There are a few important principles involved with the practice of sound healing:

Principle	Study
Resonance	Every organ, bone, and cell in the body has its own resonant frequency, your own signature vibration. Combined, these frequencies make up a cohesive frequency like the instruments of an orchestra. When a single organ in the body is out of tune, it will affect the entire body. Resonance or Sound therapy is one of the most effective methods to bring the body back into harmony, avoiding the need for drugs or surgery.
Entrainment	Nature searches for the highest state of efficiency. We see this law in action when birds fly in unison during migration, by tapping into one another's systems through subtle body language and feeling. They will flap their wings together and glide at specific altitudes timed to conserve energy, flapping

	their wings in a matching rhythm so as to take advantage of the pockets of warm air created by the bird in front of them. Humans have access to this same ability and can use it to restore bodily functions to a balanced state. If an area of our body is out of balance, we can re-tune it like we would a piano. If a piano is out of tune, do we supply it with pills or rip out the faulty strings? This is precisely what we do to the human body with modern medicine and surgery. When an individual becomes ill, some of their bodily functions are out of harmony with the body as a whole but can be put back in check with much more gentle and natural methods.
Intention	Intention is another crucial principle involved in the way sound healing works. If we sing a pure tune to another person with the right intention, then healing will be

	able to occur. Intention is not simply an action that is performed, but rather a force of meaning within the entire universe. Every action performed has a conscious or unconscious intention embedded in it. With Sound Healing treatment, the sound is the vessel for our intention in restoring harmony to the body, emotions, mind, and spirit.
Voices	The human voice is an instrument that has immense potential for healing. We all have the innate ability to produce pure vocal harmonics. Although, as we grow older, the range of our voices becomes more restricted and closed. Research has indicated that toning has a chemical effect on the body, boosting the immune system and causing the release of endorphins in the brain. Toning may also

	relieve tension during stressful situations like before surgery and can in fact lower the blood pressure and respiratory rate of cardiac patients. Toning has also shown great results in relieving insomnia and other sleep disorders.
Harmonics	Singing any note will produce harmonics and all notes are related to exact mathematical ratios. Most of the time, people are unaware of the existence of harmonics. When we find ourselves in a room with good acoustics, like a church or an amphitheater, we are suddenly aware of the richer sound, which is produced by the harmonics, the structural math of the space. Ancient civilizations used this knowledge when they constructed sacred sites like Stonehenge or the King's Chamber in the Great Pyramid. All these buildings

	had chambers where sound healing was practiced.
Intervals	When we sing several notes, one after the other, we create musical intervals. Each musical interval has different effects on our bodies, emotions, and minds. This explains why we prefer different types of music during different situations.
Chant	After a time period of singing simple chants, the mind of the singer will become more relaxed and clearer. This method is practiced in most spiritual traditions. In India, this practice is called *kirtan*. When we use repetitive phrases, we relax and reach a state of joy and inner peace. This is especially the case when we sing or chant with specific intent and intense devotion. Over time, music has become more complex in the Western society. Singers and

	musicians have to stay more focused on their left-brain functions in order to play the different parts of the music in unison. Consequently, we have lost most of the healing power of sound in modern music.
Rhythm	Slower tempo music can slow breathing rate. The human heartbeat will also match the rhythm of the music. Research showed that listening to slow, uncomplicated music lowered the heart rate and allowed for longer training sessions among young adults. Listening to hard rock music had the opposite effect, where heart rates increased, and workouts were shorter. Music influences the limbic system through pitch and rhythm, as it has an effect on emotions, feelings, and sensations. Listening to classical music can calm the nervous system and even improve metabolism.

Vibration	Everything in Nature is constantly vibrating. Our bodies even have several different rhythms.
	Heartbeat—60 to 75 beats a minute.
	Breath—14 to 16 breaths a minute.
	Cranio-sacral pulse (pressure of the fluid around the brain and down the spinal cord)—8 to 12 times a minute.
	Gastrointestinal tract (that long internal track from mouth to butt)—contracts once per minute.
	Stomach—will contract every three minutes.
	Brain wave—18 to 22 cycles per second when awake.
	Body temperature—changes depending on the different times of the day.

"**Chanting meditation**" is one of the best forms of sound healing that increases blood flow in your brain. What Hindu tradition consider as the Absolute in ancient scriptures is the divine sound of "OM". During this repetitive chant of *OM*, the electro-magnetic waves in your brain are calmed and your mind can feel very steady yet solid. The same effect is seen when using Tibetan singing bowls. Striking or rotating a mallet around the rim or body of the bowl emits specific vibrations and different frequencies are used for different healing intentions.

According to Bethiwal (2017, p.1556), "Sound and color are both characterized by frequencies. They can be used as energy techniques for balancing and aligning the chakras.". Combining the frequencies of sound (Hz) with the frequency of color (THz), accompanied by dancing, can give you a therapeutic and ethereal experience. For the third eye chakra, your focus should be to incorporate the color indigo (670-700 THz) and the musical note D# in G minor (622.25 Hz).

"Sound bathing" is another prominent practice among sound healing techniques and goes as far back as ancient Greece, where it was administered as a treatment for both physical and mental ailments. It involves completely immersing yourself in sounds and vibrations and can be done by implementing the use of several tools (as mentioned with the Tibetan singing bowls).

Tool	Description
Tibetan singing bowl	Used in ancient Buddhist practices to balance energies and promote healing.
Tuning fork	Precise tones are made by tapping the metal instrument and holding it near different areas of your body that may need healing.
Gong	Loud vibrations from the gong (frequencies that expand into open space in a geometric fashion) promote the releasing of trapped energies from the body.
Chimes	Commonly used in the practice of feng shui, wind chimes are excellent at cleansing auras.

Drum	Drums are used in ceremonies and rituals across many cultures. It is a tool that is especially efficient at improving focus and helping to tap into divine energy.
Crystal singing bowl	Made from quartz crystals, these bowls produce very specific frequencies to align with certain chakras.
Digital sound	Not necessarily as effective as the vibrations of instruments, although very prominent in the modern landscape.
Crystal pyramid	Ringing sounds are produced by striking certain parts of the pyramid-shaped quartz.

There are steps that you may want to follow before engaging in a sound bath session:

- Vibrations travel best through water and hollow spaces; therefore, it is important to ensure you are well hydrated and to only eat light meals beforehand.
- Be aware of your intentions by setting certain goals you wish to achieve after the session.
- Be sure to wear comfortable and warm clothing.

Movement Medicine

A developing practice in spiritual healing is also known as *movement medicine.* This is defined as a contemporary freestyle dance routine that allows you to interact deeply with the self, others, and the natural world. Dance can aid in self-discovery and the search for a deeper meaning, connection, and pathways that help in living life skillfully and successfully. People have varying experiences with dance. The intensity can go from ordinary to overwhelmingly strong, even life changing. Although the dance floor is not a sacred place in the sense of wider historic, religious, or social definition of worship, it may indeed become a space where the divine and sacred first appeared.

Visualization

Visualization is a trainable ability of your brain that holds several benefits. Our ability to design 3-dimensional representations of our environments showcases how our mind's visualization skills are deemed as a representation of the third eye. Active and attentive visualization, usually performed by means of artistic expression, can serve as another form of mindful meditation. Giving your brain an image, even if you are not looking at it, can still have the same internal or emotional effect of actually seeing said image. There are certain brain pathways that are formed by what we see, causing our brains to react in a certain way when envisioning that image again.

__Dreaming__

Dreaming is a way for our brains to organize new information and process experiences. By implementing the practice of dream journaling, a person can give even more structure to their subconscious thoughts and ultimately improve the ability to retrieve memories. Previously scattered thoughts, ideas, and experiences are actively stitched together and resolved.

__Breathing__

The breath is used as a gauge to determine the current state of physical and mental wellbeing. After establishing an area that needs attention, a subsequent breathing technique is used to balance the other rhythms of the body. Breathwork goes hand-in-hand with yoga postures and quiet mindfulness. It is crucial that our body receives sufficient amounts of oxygen in order to function properly, as much as the blood needs to be cleansed of carbon dioxide. In turn, breathing regulates our metabolism and vice versa.

Mala Beads

The use of mala beads (prayers beads) and yogic mantras during simple meditation have an effect on the body's circulatory rhythms and slows the breathing rate. Traditionally, the mala consists of 108 beads and one guru bead (bigger than the rest) or a tassel. By holding the string of beads in one hand, you can control your breath during meditation by doing the following steps:

- Step 1: Let the mala beads drape over your fingers in order for them to move easily.
- Step 2: Place your thumb and middle finger around the guru bead or tassel.
- Step 3: Inhale and exhale slowly (one full breath).
- Step 4: Breathe in and out while moving your fingers along each bead until you have completed the 108 full breaths.

Yogic Mantras

In terms of the yogic mantras, the most commonly used and effective one is the repetition of the phrase "*OM MANI PADME HUM*" and is referred to as the "Compassion Buddha mantra". By reciting this mantra accompanied by the use of the mala beads you can release negative energies and transform your body's frequencies. The six syllables are defined as such:

- OM—symbolizes the impure mind and body of the meditator, but, in turn, also symbolizes the pure mind and body of Buddha.
- MANI—means jewel and symbolizes the intention of the method to become enlightened with compassion and love.
- PADME—means lotus and symbolizes wisdom. The ultimate wisdom is that one realizes the emptiness of existence.
- HUM—represents an invisible and immovable unity of method and wisdom. The one is affected by the other but cannot be disturbed.

Crystals, Essential Oils, and Incense

Methods that can help us to promote physical and spiritual harmony usually involve the incorporation of crystals, essential oils, and incense. The elements present in these objects (when held, absorbed, or burnt) are ancient ingredients that may improve your body's ability to harness spiritual abilities, clear the environment of negative energies, and serve as protective shields. Certain herbs are also useful when added to a bath or tea. The following is a list of what you can incorporate during your practices.

Crystals	Essential oils	Incense	Herbs
Purple fluorite	Lavender	White sage	Lemon balm
Amethyst	Clary sage	Palo santo	Feverfew
Lapis Lazuli	Neem	Mugwort	Mint
Azurite	Myrrh	Sandalwood	Marigold
Kyanite	Peppermi	Frankinc	Dandelio

	nt	ense	n
Calcite	Lemon	Dragon's blood	Chamomile

Lucid Dream Induction

Lucid dream induction, or forcing someone to lucid dream, is a fairly common method used during therapy. This involves training the patient's brain for lucid dreaming as well as providing external stimulation. A common stimulation technique is the "reality check", where participants reflect on the question "Am I dreaming?" several times throughout the day. This mental habit can transfer into dreams and trigger the realization that one is dreaming. This habit also engages your curiosity and activates your brain's "investigative mode", leading you to distinguish what is real from what is not and to allow you to make discoveries in terms of what your inner thoughts have been silently observing.

Self-Affirmations

A technique found in both therapy sessions, as well as meditations, is the self-affirmation (or conscious auto-suggestion). By actively reminding yourself of your integrity and defined place in the world, you will not be so quick to anger and your defensive reactions towards negative feedback will be less than before. What makes this technique effective is that it is self-administered, repetitive, and carves positive perspectives into your brain's pathways. This means that instead of having rejection or insults affect you, they just roll off your back.

It also helps increase motivation to heal and grow, as you feel truly worthy of bettering yourself. The act of setting an intention and practicing a frequent repetition of positive phrases, words, and sayings will promote the transfer of powerful energy. This will ultimately aid the process of manifestation. Affirmations include, but are not limited to, complimenting yourself and actively believing that you are making the changes you wish to see in yourself. The following are a few examples of affirmations you may work into your meditation practice:

- "I am made of the same materials as the cosmos."
- "I am connected to the abundance of the universe."
- "I am connected to everyone on this planet as a being of the universe and so are they to me."
- "My soul is enlightened."
- "My aura radiates positive energy."
- "I am aligned with my purpose."
- "My courage and willpower are strong."
- "I find strength in pure light."
- "Love and peace flow through me."
- "I embrace my connection with the natural world."
- "My spirit will reach Nirvana."

Applying these techniques is essential, although it will all be in vain if you have not thoroughly cleansed your body of negative energies. There are simple changes and additions you can make to your environment, lifestyle, and habits that will help to clear any negative energy or damaging byproducts of the modern world. The rest of this sub-chapter will give insight into helpful methods.

Houseplants

A wonderful way to keep your spirit and the air pure and fresh in your home is to add houseplants to your living spaces, your bathroom, and especially your bedroom. Certain houseplants need little sunlight and can absorb harmful substances in the air, not to mention that having more living things in your home is a must to stay connected to the natural world. Purified air supports immune system function, overall mood, and restful sleep. Some options include:

- Snake plant
- English ivy
- Spider plant
- Rubber plant
- Golden pothos
- Peace lily
- Gardenia
- Love palm
- Eucalyptus branches (hang in the shower for a cleansing steam)

Himalayan Salt & Smudging

Other ways to clean your environment are by adding a Himalayan salt lamp to your bedroom (be sure to check that it is in fact made of Himalayan salt and not plastic) and practicing smudging. Himalayan salt filters the air of dust, mold, radiation from electronics, mildew, and other harmful substances. Smudging is a technique that can purify your home and body. This involves burning bundles of dried sage, cedar, or lavender and the resins of frankincense or myrrh in certain areas around your home or body. The effect is greater if you combine these practices with your meditation sessions.

Grounding

Another important practice is finding an anchor in your reality. The practice of *grounding* is often used in therapeutic sessions if you have an anxiety or paranoia disorder. As the experience of awakening a higher consciousness can be overwhelming, it is suggested that you add this technique to your daily life. It requires your attention to be directed at your senses. Focus on separating and distinguishing every environmental factor that can be perceived by your sensory instruments. This involves focusing on what you can feel (on your skin or what you may touch), what you can smell in the air, what you can see around you, and what you can hear (sounds or stillness). You undoubtedly feel a sense of calm in your awareness of the immediate surroundings.

Diet

Nourishment, nourishment, nourishment.

When we are concerned about the level of development and accessibility of our higher consciousness, we must be extremely aware of what we are putting in our bodies. You must also understand that when we talk about consuming, we are not simply talking about food. Consuming can be anything from the food we eat to the television shows we watch. The aim is to nourish your physical body as well as your soul.

The nutritional habits of modern Western society have become so fake, mass-produced, and genetically modified to the point where we cannot even call our food "food" anymore. The average Western diet contains many harmful hormones and other additives that may eventually damage your DNA. This can lead to autoimmune diseases, aggravation of cancer cells, and even diabetes. This increasingly "fake" lifestyle can even affect your brain's abilities.

For the sake of spiritual health, your diet should also consist of nutrients that will prevent or reverse that calcium buildup in the pineal gland that we discussed earlier. Your pineal gland is the organ most likely to accumulate fluoride, which leads to the formation of crystals and then hardening. The necessary production of melatonin in this gland is not only linked to your sleep patterns, but also proper immune function and a healthy cell body. Having these functions depressed causes disturbances in our body's natural rhythm. Therefore, we will have a look at foods that are rich in melatonin and those that decalcify the pineal gland.

Nuts, seeds, and root vegetables are excellent sources of the crucial vitamins and structures needed for a healthy mind. Walnuts (note the shape resembling the brain) and St. John's wort contain essential fatty acids and antioxidants that maintain healthy brain function.

Furthermore, it is found that leafy greens, raw foods, and decreased meat consumption are crucial to promote the function of your pineal gland.

For further improvement of your overall diet and to promote the growth of new nerve cells in your brain, maintain healthy DNA (without oxidative stress), and support the pineal gland, you should eat the following foods, herbs, and nutrients:

- Almonds
- Apples
- Barley
- Blueberries
- Celery
- Cherries
- Lemon juice (Great source for citric acid)
- Fennel
- Flax
- Feverfew
- Garlic
- Ginger
- Milk thistle
- Oats
- Olive oil
- Omega-3 fatty acids
- Raw apple cider vinegar
- Raw chocolate

- Red radish
- Reishi mushrooms
- Rice
- Spirulina
- Sunflower
- Tomatoes
- Turmeric
- Zinc

The pineal gland is an essential part of a complex system of organs and glands that are technically the "pacemakers" for your body's metabolism and hormone production. These "pacemakers" are influenced by exposure to light, nutrition, and movement. For the sake of nutrition in this sub-chapter, we will consider the possible benefits of the **intermittent fasting diet**.

The evolution of our human DNA was shaped during a time when food availability was not guaranteed (our ancestors leading a hunter-gatherer existence). This had an effect on our body's ability to store greater amounts of energy when food was scarce. This adaptation influenced the biological processes of our brain's metabolic and hormonal regulations. Therefore, the practice of intermittent fasting is a good option to reset the circadian rhythm of your pineal gland. By resetting, you can achieve better results in your daily diet accompanied by meditative practices.

Studies on the effect of intermittent fasting have produced surprising results in reducing stress and improving your resistance to stress all the way down your cellular level. This can improve the functionality of your brain as well as lifespan. The practice involves a diet that might restrict your calorie intake and helps you to reduce the frequency of your meals.

Intermittent fasting has several different types of restrictions that can be followed based on your personal preference, religious practices, or effect on your body type. Here is an overview of the different intermittent fasting practices for your convenience.

Type	Description
Alternate-day fasting	Involves alternating fasting days. No energy-containing foods or beverages are consumed except during the eating days.
Time-restricted fasting	Allows energy intake within specific time frames, which includes extended fasting times. Usually, this practice involves the consumption of food only

	during the later hours of your day.
Modified fasting	Allows consumption of up to 25% of your energy needs on scheduled fasting days. Involves severe energy restrictions for the first two days followed by regulated eating for five days, referred to as the 2:5 diet.
Religious fasting	Variety of practices undertaken for the purposes of religion or spirituality. The results are commonly associated with cleansing when accompanied by prayer.
Ramadan fasting	Involves fasting from sunrise to sunset during the month of Ramadan. The common practice is to consume one light meal before dawn and one larger meal after sunset.
Other religious fasts	The Church of Jesus Christ of Latter-Day Saints will fast for extended periods of time. Whereas Seventh Day Adventists will consume two meals in the first half of the day and fast for an extended nighttime interval.

Myths

A simple magical touch to the forehead during a meditation session will not fix your life. Neither is the mere repetition of the sixth chakra mantra "I believe" (which is very often used to form some kind of contact with alien life forms).

There is an abundance of websites, social media platforms, and public speakers that claim the opening of the third eye can happen within seconds and sometimes even on accident. A quick demonstration by having a group of people close their eyes and envision their third eye opening will perhaps enchant a group of spiritual newbies. However, in reality, the demonstration will be no more than a party trick.

Some people make claims that they have developed super-human skills like telekinesis or microscopic and telescopic vision after the opening of their third eye. It is undeniable that human beings can have strange and inexplicable abilities. However, there is simply no scientific or direct path that may enable a person to attain these 'skills.'

There are massive misunderstandings about achieving enlightenment. It is a case of ego still calling the shots in your mind and foolishly never thinking about being compassionate and understanding the human being. A quest for knowledge should be for the sake of bettering humankind and not the glorification of only your life. Reaching true enlightenment does not, by any means, lead to you becoming unflawed and the embodiment of the divine. What meditation and contemplation can teach us is that we are indeed flawed but not incapable of change, healing, and growth.

It is impossible to be entirely and indefinitely in control of your emotions. There are several factors in play with regards to how and why certain emotions emerge and develop. The control you seek can only be achieved on a level of better judgment. Seeking to understand and even appreciate the full range of your emotions can lead you to better manage them.

Chapter 4: Keeping Your

Third Eye Open

"The puppet is free, as long as it loves its strings." - Sam Harris

As with any achievement, the hard work will continue. Dedication and commitment are essential even before you attempt to open your third eye.

When becoming enlightened, it is a lot less likely that you will become trapped in society's negative constructs. Control of your thoughts and feelings is more in your own hands than that of a broken world. That being said, it is important to stay alert and use your new and improved intuition to differentiate between what and who is helping you grow or holding you back. Assuming a positive outlook instead, there is a whole world out there filled with like-minded individuals with whom you can form a connection. Even complete strangers can teach you things that will surprise you.

Maintaining an open third eye will require you to keep building on your relationship with the natural world. Our earth is where true spiritual energy resides. Nourish your body every day, build meaningful bonds with people as well as animals, spend time in nature, and learn as much as you can from anyone and everyone.

<u>Essential Daily Habits</u>

It is of utmost importance that we keep a close eye on our habits. Our ability to quickly form new habits can be either negative or positive. Even though we can adopt these habits quite easily, it is usually much harder to unlearn them. This is why it is important to pay attention to your daily routines, in order to develop a well-rounded healthy lifestyle. It is ultimately a healthy lifestyle that will ensure a more continuous spiritual experience.

Have a set routine that includes beneficial habits. Forming a habit is an aspect of reality that we cannot escape. It is important to keep this in mind. Being aware of this reality, we can start to observe our existing habits and their contribution to our lives or lack thereof. We need to stop and replace habits that are impacting us negatively (whether be it physically, emotionally, spiritually, or altogether) or no longer carry any significance to our lives. The best method of changing a habit is by replacing it with a new one. This is where you can hit the gold mine in terms of the progress in your pursuit of awakening. You can replace these redundant patterns of behavior with habits that will benefit you in hindsight. Take this example into consideration: you have a habit of drinking 3 beers each night. By acknowledging this, you become aware and are more likely to remove this habit from your life. You can consider the option of taking up yoga classes each night instead of drinking. They will not only improve your physical and emotional condition, but arguably also improve your financial position, since drinking everyday can start to weigh on your bank account. This is an example where the possible benefits do exceedingly outweigh the previous instant gratification.

Never underestimate the value of the great outdoors. There is a reason why people say that nature is nurture. It is crucial for us as human beings that we spend enough time in nature as a means to stabilize the mind and spirit. Equally as important is our oxygen intake and the type of physical activity that is naturally available. This will help produce endorphins, increase blood flow, and maintain the essential drainage of brain fluids. It is rather easy to find naturalists in today's age that have resorted to a mostly natural lifestyle. The reason for this renaissance is in part a result of the realization that we are in balance when we are surrounded by nature. Our senses are heightened once we set foot on any natural ground or soil; however, we are much more relaxed within. Our bodies are also physically designed to endure traveling over long distances on foot by walking (take Marco Polo as an example). The act of running was only done in short intervals, either to run away from an immediate threat or while hunting. Taking these aspects into account, it is obvious that we need to spend valuable time in nature by walking, observing, and absorbing the environment. Doing this will also complement your mindfulness/meditative practices and can help you to achieve your desired results.

Feed your mind with worthy knowledge and wisdom of truth. Learning about how the universe works, the beings that reside in it, the plants that grow, and the animals that evolve will indeed deepen your knowledge, but mostly help your compassion and perspective to grow. Being aware of everything that is possible and how little we truly know lessens our trivial worries. Continuously placing the grand scheme of things into perspective will help your brain on a biological level by improving neuroplasticity and promoting neurogenesis (the daily growth of new nerve cells in the brain).

There is a multitude of gurus, shamans, yogis, and philosophers that have been providing guidance for various practices and in-depth knowledge that have been gained from previous masters. All these practices have been documented and carried forth through this master-student relationship. These include, but are not limited to the following:

- Sam Harris (Waking Up App)—Neuroscientist, philosopher, author, and podcast host.
- Sadhguru (Jagadish Vasudev)—Yogi, author.
- Shay Jetty—Author, former monk, and life coach.
- Andy Puddicombe—Author, public speaker, and teacher of mindfulness and meditation, respectively.
- Dada Gundamuktananda—Yogic monk and meditation teacher (formerly a medical student).
- Marcus Aurelius Antoninus (Meditations book, essentially a journal of self-experience)—Roman emperor and Stoic philosopher (121-180 A.D.).

- Henry Shukman—Poet, writer, and mindfulness teacher.
- Deepak Chopra—Author and alternative medicine advocate.
- Jon Kabat-Zinn—Professor emeritus of medicine as well as the creator of "Stress Reduction Clinic" and the "Center for Mindfulness in Medicine, Health Care, and Society" at the University of Massachusetts.

There are many other teachers that are not listed above that can guide you in the journey to your awakening. It is, however, important to ensure that you select the teacher that is most suitable for your journey. Where the wisdom and knowledge of one teacher might propel you in the right direction, another might do the opposite. Be open to change and, most importantly, be honest with yourself and your intuitive feelings. With that being said, only trust these feeling once you have experienced and learned enough to understand what they tell you about yourself.

Connecting with people and animals could easily be the most crucial aspect of your life and should not be avoided. The survival of humanity has been made possible through the relationships that human beings and animals have had with one another. Through various degrees of collaboration, in our history we have accomplished unimaginable milestones that have advanced our species. Due to the technological advancements of the past century, we are nearing a dangerous situation in which we are slowly separating ourselves from others, becoming too focused on being individuals, and losing our true purpose in life. For this reason, we need to assess the way in which we use technology and how we interact with the people around us. Due to our adaptive nature, it is easy to overlook the way that we connect (or disconnect in this matter) with people and how technology impacts our lives and our relationships. If we lose the capability to communicate correctly and effectively, then we are increasing the loss of connection with humanity and we begin to diminish our existing relationships, if any. We lose sight of a necessary dynamic of reality, the playing field in which we all experience life together, although we come to play according to our own perspectives and backgrounds.

You should observe the way in which technology impacts your relationships with the people (and animals) around you. You will notice quite quickly that there is room for improvement. Once you start to do this, you will find that your relationships with the people around you will become stronger and your opportunities for new relationships will grow as well. In addition to this, your self-established beliefs and ideas will be challenged, a healthy practice for your own personal growth and knowledge.

Practice daily empathy and compassion. As a human being you have the ability to empathize with the others. While some people are better at this than others, it does not mean that you cannot practice and strengthen this skill. Before we explain this practice, it is important to understand the logic behind empathy and compassion.

Hunter-gatherers survived the harsh conditions of their reality because of their united living and social dynamics, understood and practiced by each member in the clan. Empathy and compassion played key roles in humanity's early survival, as we were much more attuned to the physical queues of ourselves and the other members of the community. Thousands of years later, we have grown more sophisticated with our social interactions and emotional intelligence. Empathy is a means of gaining perspective, as we can interpret the emotions that someone else is experiencing. Compassion is what we use to change the lives of someone that desperately requires it since we sympathize with their misfortunes. Now that you have a general understanding of empathy and compassion, you can start to apply practices on a daily basis in order to enrich your life, as well as those around you.

Listen more than you speak. Do you often find yourself speaking without end when you are in the company of other people? Once we have had our say we then *listen* to what another person has to say, all the while thinking of the next thought or idea in our mind, which we would prefer to talk about. What we fail to recognize within this process is the fact that we do not listen to what the other person is actually saying, the meaning behind their words, what they would like you to understand.

We lose two things if we proceed with this way of conversing or even absorbing information. The first is that we lose or trigger the loss of our relationships. The second loss is our selflessness and open-mindedness. When we speak to someone, we speak from our unique experiences in life and the knowledge that we have obtained through these experiences. However, this does not mean that you are always correct in your understanding and opinion on reality. Fortunately, there are others in this reality that can provide alternative experiences and perspectives that will assist you with expanding your knowledge that you can apply in your own life. The key is that you are able to listen, not just hear. Even if you disagree with the perspective of another, this can be a jumping off point in starting a healthy discussion in which everyone can benefit and grow. Try to not let your emotions control your responses. Let them subside, rationalize the situation, and then convey your thought calmly. You will be surprised how much richer your discussions and relationships will become, as well as how much easier it is to locate the negative or emotionally damaging people in your life.

Give your undivided attention. Before you can improve your attention, you must first determine the cause of your scattered or divided attention span. In our present existence, technology has become a daily part of our existence and life choices. Admittedly technology has both enriched and simplified our lives. However, what you may start to notice is that your attention span during a conversation is not so sharp. There are essentially two types of gratification: gradual gratification and instant/sudden gratification. You need to move away from instant gratification and, instead, focus on gradual gratification.

Think of a time where you labored away on a task for a prolonged period of time. While the process might have been exhausting or scary, the satisfaction you find upon finishing it is much better in comparison to the rush from instant gratification. You feel a deep sense of fulfillment and, as a result, greater motivation. This can only be achieved through extended and undivided attention to what's in front of you and what needs to be accomplished. This is also applicable to relationships (as discussed earlier in this chapter). The more time you devote to your relationship the better it will be. It is difficult in the beginning to place your undivided attention on the present situation. However, you will slowly improve this skill, as with any other. You may struggle with consistency. Ultimately, you will need to note all the distractions in your immediate environment and begin to remove them accordingly. You can spend time on social media or watch that new series that everyone is raving about if it pleases you but do so once you have done what you know is required for that day. What you will find is that you will also pay greater attention to the way you experience these small pleasures. This might bring you to the realization that you are not really interested in finishing that new series or you really don't care about Bella Hadid's new hair color. You have better things to do with your day.

Expanding your awareness of "self" can be heightened through the **practice of prayer**. This inserts your own awareness into the greater collective consciousness of your environment and community. Prayer can be understood in a religious manner or merely positive thoughts directed at the wellbeing of all living creatures. It is a way of practicing stillness and sending energy of loving-kindness into the world.

Meditation may help in the pursuit of changing your "nondual" awareness, being aware of how your thoughts and actions ripple through the universe. The perception of the "self" can range from identifying with your ego as a solitary "self" to understanding your "self" as being able to move past such limitations and have greater universal awareness. Although there is a wide range of meditative practices and philosophies within various spiritual traditions, most of them note the importance of honing this dual perception of reality, and away from your automatic ego self-identification.

Guided Practices

There are many available options regarding the guided practices led by natural healers, yogis, gurus, shamans, etc. The benefit of these practices is that you can find the ones you resonate with and incorporate them as needed into your daily routines. People are different when it comes to their level of comfort with being spiritually led. The rest of this chapter will be dedicated to your available resources for guided practices, as well as a few examples.

Yoga is defined as a practice that harnesses *pure* consciousness. It combines physical postures, breathing exercises, and spiritual contemplation to establish a union between your body and mind.

Meditation is more of an intuitional science and involves the merging of your personal awareness into cosmic awareness. We will go through examples of useful meditation and breathing techniques, their basic practice, and possible mentors that may guide you in the future.

The term meditation refers to a collection of diverse methods with the implementation of specified and intentional awareness. Recent studies have begun to show distinct results with practicing daily meditation. Although the general effects of meditation on our brains are still being debated, it is agreed by the majority of neuroscientists that brain activity is greatly improved by many forms of meditation.

Yogic, Meditative, and Contemplative Practices

Yoga Practices

Yoga type	Practice
Ashtanga	Involves a sequence of poses according to a rigid set routine that is connected to the breath.
Bikram	Consists of 26 poses that are undergone in a hot room.
Hatha	A more traditional and classic form of yoga done in a short

	time and moderate pace.
Iyengar	Focused on physical form and mental alignment, along with the use of equipment.
Restorative & Yin	Slow-paced yoga, which is done to restore the health of muscles, nerve tissue, and the nervous system.
Vinyasa	A more intense workout that involves a flowing sequence of poses and puts emphasis on the breath, usually accompanied by music.
Sahaja	An easy-to-learn combination of yoga and meditation for the general population, which promotes "thoughtless awareness".
Kundalini	A combination of repeating postures, breathing exercises, and singing or chanting.

1. Vinyasa yoga (or *Yoga Flow*) is one of the best options if you are looking to maintain a healthy mind-body harmony. Several studies have shown that this practice improves your overall health greatly. Results include the improvement of mood, cholesterol, arteries, vascular function, concentration, and control of mental activity. Students have reported increased sense of awareness, ease with the release of trapped emotions, and the ability to overcome negative habits.

Vinyasa is made up of three pillars that are posture, breath, and gaze. In all honesty, the postures in this practice can be quite challenging. Each is done in a flowing sequence, slowly moving into the next posture, coordinated with each inhale and exhale of your breath. Here is an example of a beginner Vinyasa yoga sequence for you to try:

- Step 1: Plank pose (_Kumbhakasana_)— Inhale as you come into a high push-up position, with your hands under your shoulders and feet hip-distance apart.
- Step 2: Knees-Chest-Chin pose (_Ashtanga Namaskara_)—Exhale as you lower your knees to the floor, keeping your elbows tucked in toward your sides. Keep your hips lifted off the floor but bring your chest and chin to the floor. Place your chest between your hands.
- Step 3: Cobra pose (_Bhujangasana_)— Inhale as you draw your chest forward,

keeping your hands underneath your shoulders. Extend your legs along the floor and un-tuck your toes. Draw your shoulders back and lift your chest slightly. Keep your lower ribs on the floor.

- Step 4: Downard-Facing Dog (_Adho Mukha Svanasana_)—Exhale as you lift your hips and roll over your toes, placing the soles of your feet on the floor. Ground down through your hands and the soles of your feet as you lengthen your spine. Lift your belly and sit bones to the sky.

2. Ashtanga is derived from the Sanskrit words "ashta" (eight) and "anga" (limbs), therefore "the eight limbs", which represents the path of the specific yoga routine.

- First limb (Yama): Deals with your standards, integrity, and behavior.
- Second limb (Niyama): Your self-discipline and spiritual awareness.
- Third limb (Asanas): The yogic postures. (The "primary series", explained below).
- Fourth limb (Pranayama): Your breath control.
- Fifth limb (Pratyahara) Your withdrawal and sensory transcendence, by making a

conscious effort to bring your awareness inside of yourself.

- Sixth limb (Dharana): Slowing the thinking process by bringing your concentration to a single thought, usually with the use of mantras.
- Seventh limb (Dhyana): A state of being focused and having flowing awareness.
- Eighth limb (Samadhi): This means a state of ecstasy, where you may merge focus and transcend the "self" altogether.

The primary series of Ashtanga is called *Yoga Chikitsa*, which translates into "yoga therapy" and is the foundation of the rest of the asanas. This a list of some less advanced postures if you happen to be a newcomer to the practice of yoga.

Big Toe Pose (*Padangusthasana*)

- Step 1: Stand with your feet parallel and about six inches apart. While keeping your legs straight, exhale and bend over from the hip joints, moving your torso and head as one unit.
- Step 2: Slide your middle and index fingers on each hand in-between your second and big toe. Grip your big toes by

wrapping your thumbs around the other two fingers. Press your toes down. (If you can't reach your toes while keeping your back straight, hold straps under the balls of each foot.)

- Step 3: While inhaling, lift your torso as if standing up and straighten the elbows. Lengthen the front part of your torso while exhaling. Depending on your flexibility, the lower back will hollow either more or less. Relax your hamstrings and hollow your lower belly, then lightly lift it toward the back of your pelvis.

- Step 4: Lift the top of your sternum as high as possible without lifting the head so far that the back of the neck becomes compressed.

- Step 5: During the following few inhales, lift the torso while actively contracting the front of your thighs. With each exhale lift your hips while consciously relaxing your hamstrings. As you're doing this posture, deepen the hollow in your lower back.

- Step 6: With the final exhale, bend your elbows out to the side, pull up your toes, and lengthen the front and sides of your torso, while gently lowering into a forward bend.

- Step 7: Hold the final position for one minute. Then release your toes, bring your hands to the hips, and re-lengthen the front of your torso. With your next inhale, bring your torso and head back up in a swinging motion.

The Lotus Pose (*Padmasana*)

- Step 1: Sit on the floor with your legs straight out front. Bend your right knee and bring your leg up into a cradle (the outer edge of your foot is notched into the crook of your left elbow as the knee is wedged into the crook of your right elbow, and your hands are clasped outside of your shin). Lift your torso toward the inside of the right leg so your spine lengthens. Make sure your lower back stays straight. Then rock your leg back and forth a few times, engaging the full range of movement in your hip joints.
- Step 2: Bend your left knee and turn the leg out. Rock your right leg out to the right, and then lock your knee by pressing the back of your thigh to your calf. Next, swing your leg across in front

of your torso and nestle the outside edge of your foot into the inner left groin. Press your right heel into your left lower abdomen.

- Step 3: Lean back slightly while picking your right leg up off the floor. Raise your left leg in front of the right leg by holding the underside of you left shin. Slide your left leg over the right leg, wiggling the side of your left foot deep into the right groin. Again, swing into position from your hip joints while pressing your heel against the lower abdomen and shift the sole of your foot parallel to the floor. Draw your knees very close together. Use the sides of your feet to press the groin toward the floor and lift the chest.

The Fish Pose (*Matsyasana*)

- Step 1: Lie flat on your back with your knees bent and feet on the floor. While inhaling, lift your pelvis up a bit and slide the hands (palms on the floor) below your buttocks. Rest your buttocks on the backs of the hands and tuck your forearms close to the sides of the body.

- Step 2: While inhaling again, press your forearms and elbows on the floor. Then turn your shoulder blades into your back, and with another inhale lift your chest and head up from the floor. Slowly release your head back onto the floor.
- Step 3: You may keep your knees bent or straighten your legs out onto the floor.
- Step 4: Stay like this for 15 to 30 seconds while slowly breathing. With the last exhalation, lower your chest back onto the floor. Draw your legs up to the abdomen and squeeze.

Child's Pose (Balasana)

- Step 1: Kneel on the floor. Touch your big toes together and sit on the heels, while separating your knees about as wide as the hips.
- Step 2: Lay your chest down between your thighs while exhaling. Broaden the back of your pelvis and narrow the hip points toward your navel. Lengthen your tailbone away from the rear of the pelvis while lifting the base of your skull away from the back of your neck.
- Step 3: Lay your hands on the floor alongside your upper body (palms

showing upwards) and release the fronts of your shoulders toward the floor. Feel how the shoulder blades pull back and widen across your back.

- Step 4: Stay and rest in this position for a few minutes.
- Step 5: Come up again by first lengthening your chest and then, while inhaling, lift from your tailbone by pressing down into the pelvis.

Meditation Practices

Meditation type	Practice
Vipassana	Long-term journey of meditation found within the teachings of the Buddha.
Dhyana	Also referred to as the seventh limb of yoga. It is the meditative state that evolves your intuition.

Transcendental	Involves the passive use of mantras while meditating, in order to prevent distractive thoughts. It is usually done for 20 minutes in the morning and then another 20 minutes at night.
Zen Koans	A practice that promotes creativity and poses questions beyond mere logic. Essential writings by a number of experts have been compiled and published as an extensive and apprehensive guide called "Sitting with Koans" (2006).
Loving-Kindness	Where the focus is to project wholesome and loving energy both inward towards yourself and outward towards the world.

1. **Vipassana meditation** is a highly recommended practice for those of you seeking to open your third eye and maintain spiritual enlightenment, healing, and growth. It is a mindful meditation that requires your upmost focus and awareness in order to cultivate a

calmness of the mind by stimulating an objective perspective in your thought pattern.

William Hart is an excellent guide for this method. His teachings refer to Vipassana as the development of insight, embodying the essence of the teachings of Buddha to reveal simple and effective paths to self-awareness. This is a long-term practice that increases your empathy and self-acceptance, along with reducing your heart rate and oxygen consumption. You can follow the next steps:

- Step 1: While allowing your mind to wander freely, direct your focus to the separate points as instructed. Start off with 10 minutes of focused breathing. Pay attention to the feeling of the air moving in and out of your body through the nostrils.
- Step 2: Then move your awareness to all the sensations of your body, while maintaining stillness for 15 minutes.
- Step 3: The final part is a five-minute mindfulness practice where you are required to set your focus on manifesting feelings of compassion and empathy towards all living beings.

2. Dhyana meditation (intuition meditation) is especially recommended for strengthening the abilities of your third eye. In order to hear what your deeper self has to say you need to formulate a question around what you are struggling with and then practice the following steps.

- Step 1: Spend enough time formulating your question by being as clear as possible about its intention. It is important to physically write it down in order to manifest it properly. Start by asking for help in reaching a solution to your question. You may also ask for insight during this practice.

- Step 2: Sit comfortably with a straight back (but not rigid) and closed eyes. Keep the question in your mind and repeat it to yourself a few times. Pay attention to the feelings that may arise as you do this. Note any thoughts that come up, including resistance to certain answers. Write these down as well if they seem relevant to what you need to learn.

- Step 3: Use the slow and consistent rhythm of your breath as an anchor and keep your attention on each inhale and exhale until the mind becomes more relaxed and clearer.

- Step 4: Allow your awareness to sink even deeper. You may achieve this by focusing on your heart center (the middle of your chest) or on your core center (inside of the mid-abdomen). You can also try using a visualization technique by imagining yourself descending a staircase into a peaceful valley. Focus on each individual step until you find yourself surrounded by a quiet space.

- Step 5: In this serene space, ask the Self of light and wisdom who resides in your deepest core to come forth. Otherwise, you might ask for guidance from the universe, the source of all beings.

- Step 6: Ask your question again and wait silently, without any expectation or discouragement, to see what may emerge. Keep in mind that insight does not always come in words, but it may come to you as a feeling, an image, or a seemingly external voice. Also, remember that it might not come the moment you ask for it, as intuition works according to the universe's time. Therefore, stay attentive for the next 24 to 48 hours, as answers you seek may arise during this time.

- Step 7: As the insights come to you, write them down. Keep each one in your mind and let them filter through. Note the feelings and associations that arise. You may feel the need to interpret the insights, although it is also enough just to keep it in your consciousness. As you do this, it may start morphing within your deeper consciousness by itself.
- Step 8: Finally, consider steps you can take in order to put your new insights into action. The only way to strengthen and create the habit of following your intuitive guidance is to put it to the test and be very aware of the results.

The following is another sequence that is categorized under Dhyana meditation, with the focus on practicing enlightenment through manifestation.

- Step 1: Sitting comfortably and quietly, start by becoming aware of the fact that you are aware. Your instinct will tell you that you are present, thinking, alive, and breathing. That subtle witness of your existence is the foundation of this meditation.

- Step 2: Bring a loved one to mind with whom you have a special connection and think about how you both share a consciousness within the universe. Consider how that person experiences the same emotions as you and a kinship will form by accepting that mutual awareness.

- Step 3: Now think of a person with whom you spent a brief amount of time. This person evokes no deeper emotions or opinions inside you but still try to bring to mind a thought that you shared the same consciousness.

- Step 4: Think of someone you may consider an enemy or simply dislike. Remind yourself that even though you have your differences, once again that universal consciousness exists.

- Step 5: Immerse yourself in the energies that arise. Expand those energies into the physical world around you and visualize how those energies encompass everything that exists in the universe.

- Step 6: Hold onto these thoughts and feelings. There are questions that may come up, and it is recommended that you take enough time to fully contemplate them. The immense size of the universe and the concept of oneness might be a part of this contemplation.

- Step 7: Now take your contemplation into the world of human concerns. Relate it to the daily issues you tend to fixate on or the difficult people you may have dealt with in the past or present.

- Step 8: Put this practice into your daily routine and recognize this same energy and light in other people, animals, and plants. Be observant of the effect this awareness has on your enlightened state.

Meditation does not exclusively involve step-by-step practices. Daily habits and hobbies can be a meditative practice when done with the proper awareness and completely immersing yourself in the activity. Something like baking, for example, can be meditative. You are methodically moving through the recipe, synchronizing your heartbeat with the stirring, and listening to the soothing sound of a mixer.

Breathing Techniques

Dysfunctional, shallow, or rapid breathing is a sign of your body's disrupted natural balance, in more scientific terms known as homeostasis. You may have learned about this in your elementary school science class. Losing this natural rhythm leads to a chain reaction of biochemical imbalances in your body and impairs your focus.

From our mother's womb and in early development, we gain imprinted patterns of breathing that help our bodies adapt to their ever-changing needs. Becoming more aware of your breathing creates a bridge between your unconscious and conscious mind, which can help you gain more power over your actions and allow you to manage situations (especially unexpected) with more clarity.

Breathing techniques vary from slow and mindful awareness to focused over-breathing. The technique depends on your individual needs, but the goal remains the same: to access and work through mental blockages. This opens up the possibility of having a broader perspective during your daily experiences, as well as a rhythmic flow of self-awareness. Caution! If you are prone to anxiety or panic attacks this technique may not be for you. The over-breathing technique could induce a higher heart rate and subsequent panic.

Rebirth-Breathwork

A few breathing techniques that you could regularly practice, especially as a form of therapy, are sub-categories of the "Rebirth-Breathwork" method. This method involves connected breathing accompanied by bodywork, different temperatures, and varying environments. These techniques are used to bring forth your suppressed memories and can lead to resolutions, helping you to surpass confusing mental blocks and pave the path towards your enlightenment.

One of the sub-categories is **"cold water breathwork",** which is a technique that helps us confront the natural elements and achieve better control of our undesired reactions. When your body is submerged in cold water, you experience a raise in brain activity. As you take in rapid breaths, your thoughts will start to run faster and faster through your head. Your breathing will be sporadic at the beginning, which runs at the same speed as your incoming thoughts. Your will then center your awareness on your breathing and gradually slow down your breath. You will focus on breathing in through your nose and out through your mouth. Your thoughts will start to subside, and your body's tremors and muscle contractions will start to relax. You focus on breathing deeper and deeper, allowing each action of inhaling, and exhaling to be extended. What you will find is that your body and mind will start to relax, however, clarity will emerge from and within the mind, a form of relaxed alertness. Through repetition and consistency, you will be able to observe and understand these mental and physical processes and be able to apply the same process in moments where similar reactions from the body and mind could occur.

Box Breathing

A popular breathing technique used by the Marines and U.S. Navy Seals is "Box Breathing" or "Square Breathing". This breathing technique is also used in some yogic practices. The technique is quite simple to practice and can have multiple benefits like clearing and refocusing the mind, relaxing sensations for rapid breathing, as well as lessening anxiety (also known as the fight-or-flight response). Before starting the practice, grab a timer and find a quiet, comfortable place to sit. Sit with your back straight, feet planted on the floor, and your shoulders relaxed. Set your timer for 5 minutes, close your eyes, and follow the steps below.

- Step 1: Breathe all the oxygen out of your body through your mouth. Then, breathe in through your nose while slowly counting to four in your head. Feel the sensation of your breath as you breathe in.
- Step 2: Hold the breath inside your body and slowly count to four again. Try to keep your mouth and nose relaxed. The goal is just to avoid inhaling or exhaling.
- Step 3: Breathe out while slowly counting to four. Focus on the sensation of the breath leaving your body.
- Step 4: Hold. Slowly count to four.
- Step 5: Repeat steps 1-4 until the timer relieves you of this duty. Give yourself a pat on the back.

If you find five minutes to be challenging, then reduce the time to an amount that is more suitable for you. The ultimate goal is to reach and complete at least five minutes of box breathing on a daily basis. This technique is also worth using in moments where you require some relaxation from overwhelming sensory experience or clarity of the mind.

Conqueror Breath

A breath-control technique that is accompanied by mantras is referred to as **"Conqueror Breath"** or *pranayama* (the fourth yoga limb). This technique is beginner-friendly and promotes harmony between your mind, body, and spirit. Here is how you can practice this technique.

- Step 1: Start by directing your inhales and exhales to the back of your throat. Be aware of the soft hissing sound made by this breathing technique. The hissing sound is called the *Ajapa Mantra*, which means "unspoken mantra," and it serves three purposes. It helps in slowing down your heart rate, focusing awareness on

127

your breath (preventing the mind from wandering), and regulating the consistent flow of breath.

- Step 2: Inhale through your nose. Then slowly exhale through your mouth wide open while directing the outgoing breath slowly into the back of your throat (making a drawn-out *HA* sound). Repeat a few times and then close your mouth. Then, as you inhale and exhale through the nose again, direct the breath slowly into the back of your throat once again.
- Step 3: When finished, return to normal breathing for a minute or two. Now lie down in *Shavasana* (Corpse Pose) in order to rest for a few minutes.

Chapter 5: Modern

Philosophers

"Who can live with this Consciousness and not wake frightened at sunrise?" —Allen Ginsberg

People tend to refer to ancient philosophers when discussing the guiding principles of humanity. Yet, being a "philosopher" is not a title you hear too often these days. What we don't realize is that the study of philosophy can now be found in the studies of psychology, physiology, and anthropology (with their focus on the fundamental nature of human culture and knowledge).

You should take into consideration that what these people have to say is mainly about what they have learned, experienced, or contemplated about the former. Their studies are beyond mere speculation. They have developed well-rounded theories about the human condition and those that deserve recognition are the academics that have also experienced spiritual enlightenment. Their greatest success is to have combined these strides in higher consciousness with their field of study.

Alan Watts

Alan Wilson Watts is credited with bringing Eastern philosophies into the Western world during the second half of the 20th century. His writings started with the memory of a fever-ridden dream he had when he was a child, which gave him clarity in the understanding the connection between humans and nature. Throughout his academic career, he learned the importance of a balance between the teachings of philosophies and the principles of religions. For example, he illustrated how the famous symbol of *Yin* and *Yang* is not two separate entities, but the constant dance of order and disorder that is continuously happening in our space-time continuum. It also illustrates its relevance beyond cultures to that of nature's innate balancing act. That balance is necessary for our dimension to function as it does.

"Naturally, for a person who finds his identity in something other than his full organism is less than half a man. He is cut off from complete participation in nature. Instead of being a body, he *has* a body. Instead of living and loving, he *has* instincts for survival and copulation. Disowned, they drive him as if they were blind furies or demons that possessed him." (Watts, 1962, p.8). Watts talked about how we can achieve freedom beyond the state of preoccupation, to transcend from the indoctrinated cultural mind to a unified altered consciousness. In his writings, he tried to describe what goes beyond our vocabulary, and he did so, rather spectacularly.

Watts has many published works, public speeches, and lectures that are still available across multiple platforms. In his explanation of awakening, he goes into detail about our need to have control over chaos. We tend to structure our beliefs on the concept of having order triumph over disorder. He explains that it is due to our nature of having mutually exclusive thoughts about something, meaning that we can have more than one opinion or viewpoint about a situation, but they struggle to coexist. With the implementation of Buddhist philosophy, a shift of focus can occur, and the mind can learn to comprehend the existence and necessity of both the one and the other (the dark and the light, the good and the evil, that which is within all of us and within the greater world).

Jordan Peterson

Jordan Bernt Peterson is a clinical psychologist and professor of psychology. His lectures are widely available, as well as his books and academic papers. His cultural and political viewpoints have been described in the media as conservative, although he is a firm advocate of the act of contemplation and not just accepting a viewpoint as the sole truth.

Peterson himself experienced depression and an autoimmune disorder, which led to treatment through severe pharmaceuticals that are still regarded as relatively harmless in most of Western society. He warns against the adverse effects of benzodiazepines (more commonly known as "benzos") and promotes the implementation of mindfulness, meditation, and a healthy diet instead of drugs.

In Peterson's work, *The Architecture of Belief*, he notes that our ancestors' knowledge of the cosmos as not primitive at all. He explains (2002, p.93) that the "archaic theories of creation attempted to account for the existence of the world, as experienced in totality (which means, including meaning), and not for the isolated fact of the material world. The world as experienced in totality is made up of the material things we are familiar with, and the valences we consider epiphenomenal; of the objects of experience, and the fact of the subject, who does the experiencing. The world brought into being in archaic myths of creation is phenomenological, rather than material, and includes all aspects of experience, including those things we now regard as purely subjective. The archaic mind had not yet learned how to forget what was important. Ancient stories of the generation of the world, therefore, focus on all of reality, rather than on those distant and abstracted aspects we regard as purely objective."

The point that Peterson makes is that we need to revert back to the ancient way of thinking when it comes to understanding the existence of the world and ourselves. Experience should be a concept of both the material immaterial worlds. The things we experience on a spiritual and esoteric level have just as much relevance in our scope of awareness as the simple experiences of our basic senses.

Sam Harris

Samuel Benjamin Harris is an American author, philosopher, and neuroscientist. It is also important to note that he has been practicing meditation for over 30 years after he embarked on a journey of discovery to find the answers to philosophical questions that arose during his major in English at Stanford University. He went on to study with many Tibetan, Indian, Burmese, and Western meditation teachers. Harris is deemed a controversial yet prominent figure. His writings are on various philosophical and anthropological matters, one of which is *The Moral Landscape: How Science Can Determine Human Values*. The topics he covers include, but are not limited to philosophy, neuroscience, religion, meditation, mindfulness, and free will. Harris is renowned for his secular approach to spirituality and mindfulness and has made it clear that the core components of experience such as compassion, empathy, awe, and feelings of oneness are among the most valuable experiences that we as human beings can have.

Harris has debated with philosophers, psychologists, and historians from everywhere in the world. These debates have gained him recognition throughout many fields of study, although critics both love and hate Harris (especially his views, and expressions thereof, on rationality and religion). He is the founder of the *Waking Up* app, which is intended to serve as a library of things like meditation and mindfulness. The app includes his own guided meditation practices and theoretical lessons on many subjects (free will, thoughts, compassion, the illusory self, and insights, among other subjects), as well as other valuable meditative practices from various teachers on subjects such as Stoicism, the Headless Way, The Koan Way, and much more. The *Waking Up* app was created with the main purpose of being a guide to understanding the mind (and all the components that comprise the mind) in order to live a life that is more balanced and fulfilling.

There are numerous meditation apps that teach the principles of mindfulness, however, most lack the philosophy and theory behind the practices. These practices are capable of evoking and manifesting realizations about your reality and the composition of your mind and, subsequently, your behaviors, which can have negative implications if you are not guided by the correct principles. Ultimately, Harris has placed his expertise and experiences into this app, allowing you to discover deeper fundamental aspects of your mind. These discoveries aren't merely aimed at stress reduction, but more to gain insights into reality and your subjective experiences of it. Undeniably Harris has revolutionized the way that meditation and mindfulness can be practiced and understood by anyone.

Terence McKenna

Terence Kemp McKenna was a mystic and ethnobotanist who promoted the ethical and responsible use of naturally occurring psychedelic substances. He would study, debate, and write about shamanism, anthropology, psychology, and philosophy.

In McKenna's work, "Plan, Plant, Planet," he addressed the global crisis of ignorance and denial of the self. He suggested that we, as a species, need to go back to plants to understand how to best function in this world.

McKenna is in no way promoting the use of psychedelics in his book. He is simply noting that "the solution to much of modern malaise, including chemical dependencies and repressed psychoses and neuroses, is direct exposure to the authentic dimensions of risk represented by the experience of psychedelic plants. The pro-psychedelic plant position is clearly an anti-drug position. Drug dependencies are the result of habitual, unexamined, and obsessive behavior these are precisely the tendencies in our psychological makeup that psychedelics mitigate. The plant hallucinogens dissolve habits and hold motivations up to inspection by a wider, less egocentric, and more grounded point of view within the individual. It is foolish to suggest that there is no risk, but it is equally uninformed to suggest that the risk is not worth taking. What is needed is experiential validation of a new guiding image, an overarching metaphor able to serve as the basis for a new model of society and the individual." (1998, p.6).

Chapter 6: What's Next?

"I don't think that you have any insight whatsoever into your capacity for good until you have some well-developed insight into your capacity for evil." —Jordan Peterson

Even if you have managed to open your third eye and maintain a routine of keeping it open, it is important to remember your ongoing goals and new challenges that may arise. Our main purpose in life may in fact contain multiple purposes. All of these however include continuous healing and inspiring growth in others. It may also be as simple as reaching out to your loved ones in their time of need, being kind and helpful towards other living beings, and providing the universe with your essential presence.

Achieving spiritual enlightenment requires acceptance of new realities and taking responsibility. This responsibility is the upkeep of spiritual awareness, the continued search for knowledge, and sharing experiences with other beings. It is also a responsibility towards healing your deepest wounds and working towards the evolution of your perspective. It is the acceptance of the cosmic dance of good and evil, and how everything has a purpose (even in a chaotic system). It is the acceptance of your flawed spirit and of those around you. By expanding your perspectives and your understanding of the human condition, your feeling of oneness with the universe will make sense.

How to Up Your Game?

Richard J. Davidson, the founder of the Center for Healthy Minds and a close friend of Dalai Lama, has focused his research on the basis of emotion in the brain and how meditation and contemplation can promote human flourishing. He held a conference discussing the four keys to wellbeing and came to the conclusion that we need to have a healthy outlook, practice resilience, pay attention, and engage in generosity. Living life in this way will counteract the usually negative focus points of healing the mind.

He stated (2016) that he and his colleagues published a study "where individuals who had never meditated before were randomly assigned to one of two groups. One group received a secular form of compassion training and the other received cognitive reappraisal training, an emotion-regulation strategy that comes from cognitive therapy. We scanned people's brains before and after the two weeks of training, and we found that in the compassion group, brain circuits that are important for this positive outlook were strengthened. After just seven hours—30 minutes of practice a day for two weeks—we not only saw changes in the brain, but these changes also predicted kind and helpful behavior."

With Davidson's words of wisdom in mind, try focusing on your capacity for compassion; on your outlook on life being one of kindness towards other living beings as well as yourself. You will find that the trivial issues we so easily fixate on are simply man-made obstacles in the way of creating a harmonious community that will fully appreciate how blissful life can be.

Nirvana may be reached due to the awareness of the fact that you are *able* to reach it; that it exists within our metaphysical space. Continue to set your intentions according to that awareness and begin by being kind to yourself and your own healing process.

Conclusion

"The less you open your heart to others, the more your heart suffers." —*Deepak Chopra*

Learn, heal, grow, teach, and repeat.

The more you achieve spiritual growth, the more you can expand your awareness of metaphysical space. Through this, you arrive at the conclusion that you exist as an *"us"* and not just a *"me"*. Letting go of the ego can untether your life, allowing you to become more engrossed and connected with the universe as a whole. You become more aware of your own consciousness and how it taps into the rest of the world.

It is time to thrive. Having a job and normal routines are all good and well. These things definitely serve their purpose in society and towards a sense of belonging. Still, the universe is vast, and the cosmic reality is in reach for the individuals who seek to expand their awareness. This doesn't necessarily mean that you will experience psychic visions and communicate with beings in other dimensions. It means that the swirls of milk in your coffee will seem like a work of art and every morning this will bring you an appreciation for the small beauties of the world. Have a peace of mind at all times. The goal is to learn to appreciate being present, being alive, being able to merely exist in this beautiful universe.

Good luck with your spiritual journey, and may you find a purpose, loving-kindness, immense wisdom, and true enlightenment.

References

400 Albert Einstein Quotes That Will Move (And Surprise You). (2017, November 8). https://wisdomquotes.com/albert-einstein-quotes/

Alan Watts Explains What Awakening Means. (n.d.). Www.youtube.com. Retrieved August 1, 2021, from https://youtu.be/7SfZZlpfaNo

Alexandra Mackenzie. (2020, October 26). *Ashtanga Yoga Poses: A Beginner's Guide to the Primary Series.* YOGA PRACTICE. https://yogapractice.com/yoga/ashtanga-yoga-poses/

Allen Ginsberg Quotes (Author of Howl and Other Poems) (page 2 of 11). (n.d.). Www.goodreads.com. Retrieved July 31, 2021, from

https://www.goodreads.com/author/qu
otes/4261.Allen_Ginsberg?page=2

Andrew Ferebee. (2019, November 14).
*10 Sam Harris Quotes to Help You
Make Sense of a Crazy World -*.
Knowledge for Men.
https://www.knowledgeformen.com/be
st-sam-harris-quotes/

Cahn, B. R., Delorme, A., & Polich, J.
(2009). Occipital gamma activation
during Vipassana meditation. *Cognitive
Processing*, *11*(1), 39–56.
https://doi.org/10.1007/s10339-009-
0352-1

Caldwell, C., & Victoria, H. K. (2011).
Breathwork in body psychotherapy:
Towards a more unified theory and
practice. *Body, Movement and Dance in
Psychotherapy*, *6*(2), 89–101.
https://doi.org/10.1080/17432979.2011.
574505

Capozziello, N. (2017, May 19). *One
culture's crazy is another culture's wise*

| *Crosscut*. Crosscut.com.
https://crosscut.com/2017/05/crazywis
e-siff-phil-borges-kevin-tomlinson
Carr, M., Konkoly, K., Mallett, R.,
Edwards, C., Appel, K., & Blagrove, M.
(2020). Combining presleep cognitive
training and REM-sleep stimulation in a
laboratory morning nap for lucid dream
induction. *Psychology of
Consciousness: Theory, Research, and
Practice*.
https://doi.org/10.1037/cns0000227
de-Wit, P. A. J. M., Dias-de-Oliveira, C.
A., Costa, R. V. da L., Cruz, R. M., &
Menezes, C. B. (2019). Uma exploração
do processamento de memorias
suprimidas durante Rebirthing
Breathwork. *Revista Brasileira de
Psicoterapia, 21*(1).
https://doi.org/10.5935/2318-
0404.20190005

Dr. Jordan Peterson. (2019). *Jordan Peterson*. Jordan Peterson. https://www.jordanbpeterson.com/

Dr. Richard Davidson TEDx: How Mindfulness Changes the Emotional Life of our Brains. (2020, August 10). Healthy Minds Innovations. https://hminnovations.org/blog/learn-practice/richard-davidson-tedx

Gage, F. (2001). *Neurogenesis in the Adult Brain*.

Gheban, B. A., Rosca, I. A., & Crisan, M. (2019). The morphological and functional characteristics of the pineal gland. *Medicine and Pharmacy Reports*, *92*(3), 226–234. https://doi.org/10.15386/mpr-1235

Goalcast. (2017, July 4). *Top 44 Deepak Chopra Quotes to Inspire Your Inner Wisdom*. Goalcast. https://www.goalcast.com/2017/07/04/top-44-deepak-chopra-quotes-to-inspire-your-inner-wisdom/

Haupt, S., Eckstein, M. L., Wolf, A., Zimmer, R. T., Wachsmuth, N. B., & Moser, O. (2021). Eat, Train, Sleep—Retreat? Hormonal Interactions of Intermittent Fasting, Exercise and Circadian Rhythm. *Biomolecules*, *11*(4), 516. https://doi.org/10.3390/biom11040516

Heather, S. (2007). WHAT IS SO UND HEALING? *Wholistic Healing Publications*, *7*(3).

Hejazi, M. (2005). Geometry in nature and Persian architecture. *Building and Environment*, *40*(10), 1413–1427. https://doi.org/10.1016/j.buildenv.2004.11.007

How to Do a Vinyasa in Yoga. (2014, April 12). YogaOutlet.com. https://www.yogaoutlet.com/blogs/guides/how-to-do-a-vinyasa-in-yoga

https://www.facebook.com/fearlessmotivationofficial. (2017, June 18). *21 Friedrich Nietzsche Quotes That'll*

Change The Way You Think. Fearless Motivation - Motivational Videos & Music. https://www.fearlessmotivation.com/20 17/06/18/friedrich-nietzsche-quotes/

Hyman, M. (2007). Alternative Therapies in Health and Medicine. (Altern Ther Health Med. *Alternative Therapies in Health and Medicine, 13*(5), 10–11.

Inner peace. Inner Hope with Dada Gunamuktananda #isharehope Episode 111. (n.d.). I Share Hope. Retrieved July 26, 2021, from http://www.isharehope.com/interviews /inner-peace-inner-hope-with-dada-gunamuktananda-isharehope-episode-111/

inspiringquotes.us. (2019). *Top 30 quotes of TERENCE MCKENNA famous quotes and sayings | inspringquotes.us*. Inspiring Quotes.

https://www.inspiringquotes.us/author/4469-terence-mckenna

Iqbal, M. (2013, July 21). The "third eye" connection. *The Hindu.* https://www.thehindu.com/sci-tech/health/the-third-eye-connection/article4932128.ece

Khalsa, D. S., Amen, D., Hanks, C., Money, N., & Newberg, A. (2009). Cerebral blood flow changes during chanting meditation. *Nuclear Medicine Communications, 30*(12), 956–961. https://doi.org/10.1097/mnm.0b013e3 2832fa26c

Kieft, E. (2014). Dance as a moving spirituality: A case study of Movement Medicine. *Dance, Movement & Spiritualities, 1*(1), 21–41. https://doi.org/10.1386/dmas.1.1.21_1

Korkmaz, A., Reiter, R., Tan, D., & Manchester, L. (2011). Melatonin; from pineal gland to healthy foods. *Spatula DD - Peer Reviewed Journal on*

Complementary Medicine and Drug Discovery, 1(1), 33. https://doi.org/10.5455/spatula.201101 13080358

Krygier, J. R., Heathers, J. A. J., Shahrestani, S., Abbott, M., Gross, J. J., & Kemp, A. H. (2013). Mindfulness meditation, well-being, and heart rate variability: A preliminary investigation into the impact of intensive Vipassana meditation. *International Journal of Psychophysiology, 89*(3), 305–313. https://doi.org/10.1016/j.ijpsycho.2013. 06.017

Kyrah, M., & Daniels. (2016). *The Coolness of Cleansing: Sacred Waters, Medicinal Plants and Ritual Baths of Haiti and Peru.*

Mano, H., & Fukada, Y. (2006). A Median Third Eye: Pineal Gland Retraces Evolution of Vertebrate Photoreceptive Organs. *Photochemistry and Photobiology.*

https://doi.org/10.1562/2006-02-24-ir-813

Manocha, R. (2000). Why meditation? *Australian Family Physician, 29*(12).

MATTSON, M., & WAN, R. (2005). Beneficial effects of intermittent fasting and caloric restriction on the cardiovascular and cerebrovascular systems. *The Journal of Nutritional Biochemistry, 16*(3), 129–137. https://doi.org/10.1016/j.jnutbio.2004.12.007

Meah, A. (2019, August 21). *50 Inspirational Jordan Peterson Quotes On Success | AwakenTheGreatnessWithin*. Awaken the Greatness Within. https://www.awakenthegreatnesswithin.com/50-inspirational-jordan-peterson-quotes-on-success/

Miller, T., & Nielsen, L. (2015). Measure of Significance of Holotropic Breathwork in the Development of Self-

Awareness. *The Journal of Alternative and Complementary Medicine*, 21(12), 796–803.
https://doi.org/10.1089/acm.2014.0297

Mills, P. J., Peterson, C. T., Pung, M. A., Patel, S., Weiss, L., Wilson, K. L., Doraiswamy, P. M., Martin, J. A., Tanzi, R. E., & Chopra, D. (2018). Change in Sense of Nondual Awareness and Spiritual Awakening in Response to a Multidimensional Well-Being Program. *The Journal of Alternative and Complementary Medicine*, 24(4), 343–351.
https://doi.org/10.1089/acm.2017.0160

National Geographic Society. (2019, August 19). *Hunter-Gatherer Culture*. National Geographic Society.
https://www.nationalgeographic.org/encyclopedia/hunter-gatherer-culture/

Patterson, R., & Sears, D. (2017). Annual Review of Nutrition Metabolic Effects of Intermittent Fasting. *Annual Review of*

Nutrition.
https://doi.org/10.1146/annurev-nutr-071816-

Piña, A. A., Shadiow, J., Tobi Fadeyi, A., Chavez, A., & Hunter, S. D. (2021). The acute effects of vinyasa flow yoga on vascular function, lipid and glucose concentrations, and mood. *Complementary Therapies in Medicine, 56*, 102585. https://doi.org/10.1016/j.ctim.2020.102585

Qasrawi, S. O., Pandi-Perumal, S. R., & BaHammam, A. S. (2017). The effect of intermittent fasting during Ramadan on sleep, sleepiness, cognitive function, and circadian rhythm. *Sleep and Breathing, 21*(3), 577–586. https://doi.org/10.1007/s11325-017-1473-x

Raypole, C. (2019, November 11). *How to Use Mala Beads For Meditation.* Healthline.

https://www.healthline.com/health/how-to-use-mala-beads#how-to-use

Rinpoche, Z. (n.d.). *The Benefits of Chanting OM MANI PADME HUM - FPMT*. Fpmt.org. https://fpmt.org/education/teachings/lama-zopa-rinpoche/the-benefits-of-chanting-om-mani-padme-hum/

Robin Williams Quotes. (n.d.). BrainyQuote. Retrieved July 26, 2021, from https://www.brainyquote.com/authors/robin-williams-quotes

Sam Harris | Home of the Waking Up Podcast. (2019). Sam Harris. https://samharris.org/

Sushma, G., Bane, B., Rele, U., Nrityalaya, S., & Sanshodhan, E. (2021). *A)-Nalanda Nrityalaya Kala Mahavidyalaya Ph.D research scholar Principal, Nalanda Nritya kala Mahavidyalaya, Certified Yoga Instructor -Yoga Vidya Niketan*.

Tan, D., Xu, B., Zhou, X., & Reiter, R. (2018). Pineal Calcification, Melatonin Production, Aging, Associated Health Consequences and Rejuvenation of the Pineal Gland. *Molecules*, *23*(2), 301. https://doi.org/10.3390/molecules23020301

Tang, Y.-Y., Hölzel, B. K., & Posner, M. I. (2015). The neuroscience of mindfulness meditation. *Nature Reviews Neuroscience*, *16*(4), 213–225. https://doi.org/10.1038/nrn3916

Tarrant, J. (2018, September 7). *How to Practice Zen Koans*. Lion's Roar. https://www.lionsroar.com/how-to-practice-zen-koans/

Tay, K., & Baldwin, A. L. (2015). Effects of Breathing Practice in Vinyasa Yoga on Heart Rate Variability in University Students- A Pilot Study. *Journal of Yoga & Physical Therapy*, *05*(04). https://doi.org/10.4172/2157-7595.1000214

Walker, R. F., McMahon, K. M., & Pivorun, E. B. (1978). Pineal gland structure and respiration as affected by age and hypocaloric diet. *Experimental Gerontology, 13*(3-4), 91–99. https://doi.org/10.1016/0531-5565(78)90001-3

Yoga Journal - Yoga Poses, Classes, Meditation, and Life - On and Off the Mat - Namaste. (2019). Yoga Journal. https://www.yogajournal.com/